THE GREY CUP STORY

To Mister Greg.

THE
GREY CUP
STORY

*The dramatic history
of football's most
coveted award*

By

Jack Sullivan

A Christopher Ondaatje Publication

PAGURIAN PRESS LIMITED
TORONTO

Distributed by
Burns & MacEachern Limited
62 Railside Road, Toronto, Canada
Distributed in the U.S.A. by Stephen Greene Press, Brattleboro, Vermont

Library of Congress Catalog Number: 74-133790
ISBN 0-919364-04-7

Printed and Bound in Canada

CONTENTS

CHAPTER I

SYMBOL OF CONTROVERSY

The Grey Cup started life three months behind schedule because a sports-minded, aristocratic Englishman suffered a temporary lapse of memory. He forgot to have the Cup fashioned but did so after receiving a gentle, diplomatic nudge from Cup trustees.

In the agony of its formative years it lived much like a call girl: pampered, then ignored, coddled, then forgotten. The trophy was donated in 1909 for the "amateur rugby football championship of Canada" by Earl Grey, one of Canada's most popular governors-general who served an extended term from 1904 to 1911 and who died Aug. 29, 1917, at his home in England.

Albert Henry George Grey, the fourth Earl, liked to slip away from his chores at Government House to watch football at Ottawa's Varsity Oval and it was his fancy to leave in Canada some memento of his love of the game.

The Cup has been lost and stolen. One in 10,000 Canadians would not recognize it if it landed on their kitchen table. Criticize it and little old ladies from Spuzzum, B.C., to Twillingate, Newfoundland, who normally would not know a punt from a pass, will ostracize you as a person against motherhood, roast beef and apple pie.

The Cup has spawned national football heroes, goats and beauty queens. It has put frightened politicians on horses, spurs and ten-gallon hats on drugstore cowboys and millions of usually-placid Canadians in front of television sets to roar at the organized mayhem by men in padded uniforms thirsting to get their grubby, bandaged or bloodied hands on it to drink champagne from its silver lips.

Possibly no other sports trophy in existence can match the career of this $48 undistinguished 18-inch-high mug. It was disdained by Western teams of an early era who wouldn't take a train ride to play for it until they had settled what they considered a much more important issue: which railway line to take to the site of the game. Invariably, when agreement was reached between feuding players and team officials, the governing Canadian Rugby Union said no dice; it is too late in the season for an East-West final.

It was ignored by Western teams who decided to pass up the chance to play for the Cup when they had to wait weeks while the East conducted its playoffs leading to a berth in the classic. It suffered through the indifference of sports writers who didn't refer to it by name. For the first 25 years or more of its existence, and even after the West first challenged for it in 1921, the Grey Cup final was called the Canadian championship or Canadian final. That's what sports writers called it in the 1909-1920 era when only three football unions — the Big Four, the Ontario Rugby Football Union and the Intercollegiate — met for what properly should have been called the Eastern final. To Eastern critics, Canadian football extended from Montreal in the East to Hamilton in the West.

And when the West finally did make it a truly national final, its clubs had to travel to Toronto, Hamilton, Ottawa, Kingston, Sarnia, Montreal or wherever the CRU decided the contest would be played. Western challengers were referred to as intermediates, the finals a farce and one Eastern critic wrote that "something must be done to stop these fiascos." If ever the West had reason to throttle the East on a football field, its players and officials had only to glance at the sports pages of those Eastern daily newspapers in the early 1920s.

The Cup has been won and lost by Canadians who bought their own uniforms for the privilege of being able to play on a brisk autumn Saturday afternoon and by well-paid American and Canadian players, coached by handsomely-paid Americans on teams with annual budgets of close to a million dollars. It has been won and lost by tough, keen-eyed young men living in the host city who walked or took a street car to the stadium on Cup final day from their homes or from work, sucked oranges or gulped soft drinks in post-game dressing room celebrations and who returned to their normal, every-day existence. No fuss and, many times, no Cup.

But who cared? Maybe they would get together for a victory celebration, receive a cricket cap, a crest, a ring or a jacket. This was dictated by the club's finances and many times officials had to scrape to get

8

together $75 or $100 to spend on these souvenirs. A couple of stars on a Cup-winning club during the Second World War were handsomely rewarded. One received a kitchen stove for his wife, the other a coat of imitation fur for his spouse.

Warren Stevens, quarterback of the Montreal Amateur Athletic Association club that won the 1931 final, found a $20 bill tucked in his shoe after the game. Another player in the early forties received $15, two pounds of butter and a pound of tea.

Now, Canadian and American football player-businessmen arrive at the host city by jet a few days before the kickoff, stop at expensive hotels, study game films of their opponents, and gather for endless skull sessions. Workouts are held in secret and a royal commission would be set up if it ever leaked out that the quarterback had a hang nail or that a swift tight end had stubbed his toe.

Eastern bookmakers almost annually call the East to win. But for the true football fan it is East versus West and "may the best team win." The Cup final means, among many things, lost weekends for those who make too many pub stops, TV instant replays if you don't get it the first time, post-mortems, winter-long arguments. And money.

Every member of the winning team receives $1,500 plus a built-in argument for a fatter contract next year and, to a few of the more glamorous, a chance to peddle automobiles, shaving cream, razor blades, deodorants, hair dressing, or energy food on TV.

The Cup has prompted player raidings from teams in the United States, court cases, undeclared wars between leagues of the two countries and financial windfalls by airline companies who airlift muscled young men to football camps from Montreal to Vancouver at the press of a panic button.

The search for the Cup has shot annual team budgets from a few hundred dollars to nearly $1,000,000. Ticket prices have risen to $15 from 25 cents, radio broadcast rights to $70,500 from $100, Cup program rights to nearly $20,000 from absolutely nothing, gross gate receipts to more than $400,000 from a sickly $1,798 in 1940, television rights to $199,000 from around $7,500 and film rights to $35,000 from zero.

There is nothing pedestrian about the Cup final, including the status of the coaches. Win or lose, coaches who bring their teams to a World Series, the Football Association Cup, or a Stanley Cup usually can count on a raise and a new contract. But in four straight years — from

1950 to 1953 — Western coaches who made it to the Cup final knew before the game that they were out of a job.

Politicians have made emotional speeches about how the Grey Cup has "brought East and West together in a spirit of harmony and good-will." And it has resulted in bitter wrangling between Eastern and Western football officials and, on one occasion in the early 1950s, a fist-swinging incident in a Toronto hotel room involving an official of the ORFU and a representative from the Western Conference.

Grey Cup week has been built up as a festival of fun, sportsmanship, parties, beauty queen contests, parades featuring high-stepping, bare-legged girls with their goose pimples showing, bands, chuckwagons, horses, fiddlers, floats. And it has resulted in a weekend police haul of nearly 700 roisterers charged with drunkenness, vandalism, or assault, whose idea of fun was to smash store windows, tear down street decorations, belt innocent bystanders and throw mattresses and other bric-a-brac out of hotel room windows.

Ticketless fans have broken down fences, piled up five and 10 deep around sidelines and dared police to move them. Other years, would-be fans stayed home at the slightest hint of rain, snow, freezing temper-atures, high winds or when they were fairly certain that the final would be a one-sided contest.

In 1929, the Cup final at Hamilton presented the picture of about 100 clumps of ice, identified as almost frozen fans, sitting in the stands to peek out at equally frozen men performing all sorts of unrehearsed stunts on a field of ice. Thirty-four years later at Toronto, a mob of nearly 33,000 paid up to $10 a seat for a game played in a huge bowl of fog.

Cup finals have been watched by top-hatted dandies and their ele-gantly dressed ladies sitting in open carriages lined up along the side-lines; or by daring youths perched precariously on limbs of trees and on nearby rooftops. Two men rode to the 1953 final in a hearse and people will swear to this day that intoxicated onlookers outside the stadium took the pledge as the occupants, merry-eyed and light of step, clambered out.

Len Back, a legend in Hamilton and club manager for more than 40 years, tossed the Cup in the hall closet of his home in 1929 where it was used as a receptacle for galoshes and umbrellas. Len didn't bother to bring it out after the Tigers won the Cup that year and no one missed it. It was locked in a trust company vault in Toronto and

10

forgotten by a Cup trustee during the First World War years. In 1920, a member of the family noticed it among the heirlooms and told his brother to "get that thing out of here."

It was the only survivor of a disastrous fire that swept through the clubhouse of the Toronto Argonaut Rowing Club in March, 1947. Other valuable trophies were melted down and ruined by the heat and flames and there, nothing more than smoke-blackened, was the Cup hanging on a nail jutting out of a still-smouldering wall.

University of Toronto Blues, three-straight winners from 1909 to 1911, arbitrarily said it was theirs until someone came along and beat them in the Cup final. They made it stick. The Blues didn't make it to the final again until 1914, lost 14-2 to Toronto Argonauts, and reluctantly turned it over.

Another college team, McGill Redmen from Montreal, refused to challenge for it. The team qualified for a Cup final berth first in 1912 and the players advised fellow students and faculty members that they wouldn't play because "we can't afford the time away from our studies."

Referee Phil MacKenzie worked the 1910 final for his Montreal-Hamilton return train transportation costs. He turned down the $50 fee, saying it was an honor to officiate in a Cup final. Referee Hec Crighton of Toronto saved a player from drowning in full sight of 27,000 fans at the famous 1950 Mud Bowl by plucking him out from a face-first position in the mud.

And the Cup's birthdate, indelibly etched on the trophy, is wildly inaccurate. Hamilton Tigers, 1915 Cup winners, decided at one apparently wild celebration during the long winter months that they had been cheated out of a place in history. They had won the Canadian championship in 1908, figured this deserved suitable recognition and hired a silversmith to record the victory on the trophy.

Ted Reeve, respected Toronto Telegram sports columnist and a one-time football great, summed up Cup-winning enthusiasm for the players of his generation when he wrote in the 1950s that "for all we know, the victory party is still going on." That was written more than 20 years after the Moaner, as he is affectionately known, and his Toronto Balmy Beach club had won the Cup in 1930.

Probably the most notable absentee during victory celebrations in the long history of the Cup was coach Teddy Morris of Toronto Argonauts. Teddy was nowhere in sight during the club's finest hour in 1947 after guiding the team to its third straight victory over Winnipeg

Blue Bombers. He was nursing a sick horse on his suburban Toronto farm.

High up among the tall Cup yarns is one centred around the Winnipegs, the first Western winner in 1935. Winnipegs didn't have enough money to get out of Hamilton until Les Isard, a club executive, paid their hotel bill. British Columbia Lions spent nearly a million dollars to win the trophy in 1964, and left it in a Toronto hotel room when they checked out. An official hustled back in a taxi, retrieved it and made it to the airport before the team plane took off.

Calgary Tigers talked about a Cup challenge as far back as 1911 but it took an anonymous letter writer to get an East-West meeting on the rails 10 years later. Billy Foulds, Canadian Rugby Union president at the time, received the letter and moved into action. He arranged the 1921 national final and put up $4,000 of his own money to help make the first East-West game possible.

Within 20 years, East and West were locked in disputes mainly concerning import quotas and regulations, playing rules and the unsavory fact that the West had little to say in the East-dominated CRU. In those early days the East called the tune and the West danced.

And Eastern sports writers helped widen the rift. When Edmonton Eskimos made the first Western Cup challenge and Edmonton Elks followed in 1922, Eastern writers said they were "gallant" but outclassed. As the challenges continued, the shafts from Eastern critics became more pronounced. The Westerners were termed "intermediates" and, by Eastern standards, they probably were.

But the East overlooked one fact of life. It was hip-high in Canadian talent with the Big Four, Intercollegiate and ORFU Unions and junior and intermediate leagues, while the West was forced to bolster its club strength with brawny Americans who crossed the border in search of a job and, for kicks, a spot on a team with maybe, a few dollars spending money.

The Eastern attitude nettled the Westerners and all of this probably was stored in the mind of Coach Al Ritchie of Regina Roughriders. He took Roughrider clubs east four consecutive years, 1929 to 1932. His players knew every whistle stop along the way from Regina to Toronto, Hamilton, Kingston, Montreal. But, no wins.

Shortly before his death in 1966, Ritchie recalled these early years. "I knew that Roughriders didn't stand much of a chance but I envisioned the day when the West would win the Cup. I felt we just had

12

to keep challenging for the trophy." Ritchie, as much as any football official in the country, helped make the Grey Cup as it is today.

Finally, on Dec. 7, 1935, the West took dead aim and let the East have it on a football field. Ironically, Ritchie wasn't at the old Hamilton Amateur Athletic grounds for the occasion. He and his Roughriders were back in Regina when the Winnipegs beat Hamilton Tigers 18-12 and Western football players and fans relished every lip-licking minute of it.

This was the glorious day when the West smelled blood, Fritzie Hanson streaked up and down the field like a guy with a hotfoot and the Grey Cup shed its anonymity. This was the day when the almost-forgotten trophy became 10 feet tall. This was the day when newspapers "discovered" the Grey Cup.

The skies over Hamilton were overcast and the field was slippery. But to the few Westerners in the crowd of 6,405 the sun was blazing, the field was dry and every blade of grass was a beautiful paddy green in color, matching the complexions of the downhearted Tiger fans.

And if the Cup was 10 feet tall, make that 20 feet for Coach Bob Fritz and every one of his players. Youngsters in Western Canada probably were not aware that Hanson was known to his mother as Melvyn, but it didn't take them long to find out his shirt size and what he ate for breakfast.

This was the day that gave Lou (Rosy) Adelman, a hulking Winnipegs lineman, great knuckle-cracking satisfaction. He was the only holdover from the 1925 Winnipeg Tammany Tigers who had lost 24-1 to the Senators at Ottawa and Rosy memorized everything the Eastern critics had written about the contest and the Western challengers.

"This game was a joke," said one. "Winnipeg was in about the intermediate class as far as Eastern ranking goes," wrote another. But this was 1935 and Fritzie and Rosy and other Winnipegs players didn't know, and undoubtedly didn't care, that club officials were faced with a bit of a problem before they departed from Hamilton and an incredulous and unbelieving Eastern Canada.

Gate receipts had totalled $5,583.92, plus $100 for radio broadcasting rights, and Winnipegs' share wasn't enough to cover expenses. Treasurer G. Sydney Halter, later to become the first commissioner of Canadian professional football, met with club executives on the scene and Les Isard picked up the hotel tab.

Within a year, jubilation gave way to frustration for the West and, again, an ironic twist was added. Ritchie's Regina Roughriders had tumbled Winnipeg off the Western throne and they were not allowed to take part in the 1936 Cup final. Western hands reached for Eastern throats. "You can't take it," Westerners told Eastern officials. "We whipped you on the football field and you hammer us in the committee rooms."

The issue revolved around American imports. Winnipegs had won the Cup in 1935 with seven on its roster and the CRU, with backing from the Big Four, ORFU and the College unions, decided to stiffen regulations concerning the use of Americans and the West didn't go along with the ruling in its league and playoff games. The CRU said in March, 1936, that only American residents of Canada before Jan. 1 that year were eligible to play. The CRU ruled that the Roughriders had five ineligible imports on its roster and said there would be no East-West final.

Regina officials volunteered to drop them. "Too late," said the CRU. "Let them declare their cheese champions if they want to," Ritchie declared. Result: Ottawa Roughriders, Big Four champions, met Sarnia Imperials of the ORFU for the trophy. It was to be another 15 years before a Regina club won the Western title and qualified to meet the East. By that time, in 1951, Al Ritchie was no longer at the helm.

The 1936 East-West feuding was still lingering when another fight developed in 1937. This time it was over playing rules. The West wanted extended zones of blocking for linemen to 10 yards from three yards to apply in all senior football unions. The CRU rules committee ruled against the move although the West played the 10-yard blocking in its league and playoff games. Finally, in 1938, the CRU gave the West two years to get in line or forget about a berth in the Cup classic.

The West continued with the 10-yard blocking in 1939, and Winnipeg Blue Bombers travelled to Ottawa, defeated the Rough Riders 8-7 in a wild game. To show how versatile they were, the Bombers accomplished victory by adhering to the CRU's three-yard blocking rule.

Again, in 1940, the West stuck to its extended blocking in its own conference and the CRU ruled no East-West final. Committee-room verbal battles broke out. The West offered to play the East with proceeds going to war charities and, once again, the CRU said no. Instead, the CRU scheduled an unprecedented two-game total-point all-Eastern Cup final between the Big Four champion Ottawa Rough Riders and ORFU champion Toronto Balmy Beach. It was a crashing flop at the

14

gate with an all-time record low of 1,700 paid admissions for the second match at Ottawa and gate receipts of only $1,798, the lowest on record.

War charities received $32 and 82 street car tickets as their share of the receipts. The $32 was in the kitty after game expenses were paid and the trolley tickets turned up when the hat was passed in the stands. The West pulled out of the CRU. James Bannerman of Calgary, CRU president, resigned. Finally, in 1941, they patched up their differences to indulge in East-West wartime play .

All this time the West was trying to prove an obvious point. Open up the game with the extended blocking and the forward pass, get rid of the archiac two-bucks-and-a-kick style of play and spectators in increasing numbers will knock at the ticket-selling windows.

Long-memoried Western fans recalled the fuss made by the CRU when the West first introduced the pass into the Canadian game in 1929. The West went all out with the new weapon but the East, and the CRU, said the pass could not be thrown inside the defensive team's 25-yard line. This was the way the East employed the pass in 1929 and 1930 and the bob-tailed version was allowed in the Cup finals those two years. The CRU finally ruled in 1936 that the pass could be thrown from anywhere on the field.

It took a lot of talking from the West to get their Eastern counterparts around to their way of thinking. The Eastern clubs, with large populations to draw from and with long lines of players trying to make it to the Big Four and the strong ORFU, were in good financial shape. The fans were knocking at their doors, so why change.

With the end of the Second World War football started to build up in the West and suddenly, in 1948, the Cup final became the greatest sports event in the country. The architects in the change were a Calgary alderman who decided it was time to throw a party that the East, specifically Toronto, would never forget, and Calgary Stampeder Coach Les Lear.

Calgary had made it to the Cup final for the first time and Alderman Don MacKay said it was time to inject some color into the event. Hundreds of cowboy-garbed citizens from the foothills city arrived in Toronto three days before the kickoff and hammed it up on Toronto streets with horses, chuckwagons, flapjacks, impromptu parades and dances.

They roamed the streets in their ten-gallon hats, high boots and spurs. They hoisted Toronto mayor Hiram (Buck) McCallum onto a horse.

15

Hotel managers ordered their lobbies cleared of all movable furniture, flower pots and assortment of odds and ends. Downtown pubs were packed with celebrating Westerners in the red and white colors of the Stampeders — and gawking Easterners. Stampeder fans probably broke every liquor law in Ontario and the police, caught up in the festival atmosphere, looked the other way.

It was all fun and games, nothing like the rowdyism associated with the final in later years, particularly when the game was played in Vancouver. Meanwhile, at a highway dine-and-dance place known as the Pig 'n Whistle, 35 miles west of Toronto, Lear whipped his collection of old pros and tough, junior-aged kids into top shape. They had been undefeated in the 12-game WIFU schedule and made it past Saskatchewan in the Western playoffs.

Stampeders didn't impress Easterners, and the Ottawa Rough Riders were 5-to-1 favorites. It was an established betting pattern in East-West play and it continued for years, even when Edmonton Eskimos beat Montreal Alouettes three straight starting in 1954 and when Winnipeg Blue Bombers defeated Hamilton Tiger-Cats with some regularity in the late 1950s and early 1960s. For the record, 42 East-West Cup finals have been held from 1921 through 1969 and the West has won only 13. But, in the 21 meetings since 1948, the West has won nine times.

At the moment, though, in 1948, the odds didn't mean a thing to the Stamps or their wild supporters. They only cared about what the scoreboard had to say at the end of the game. It read: Calgary 12 Ottawa 7.

The West had won and just about all of Canada blew its top. Everyone, it seemed — except Ottawa fans — loved those uninhibited Stampeder fans who proved that you can mix up a few hundred Easterners and Westerners and everyone can have a good time. Edmonton, Winnipeg and Regina clubs had made losing pilgrimages east in the past and other Winnipeg clubs had won in 1935, 1939 and 1941. But these were what might be called cold-blooded affairs.

The teams were accompanied by a few stragglers who checked in at a hotel overnight, watched the game and headed home to the friendly confines of the West. They were faces in the crowd. Nothing more. In 1948, the Cup became a different breed of cat—with a colorful, exciting byplay by Westerners who had nothing to celebrate really until the kickoff except that their heroes had made it to the big game.

16

But Cup watchers realized that a little-known Calgary alderman had deposited a million-dollar baby in the CRU's lap. A win or loss for the Stampeders didn't matter. The win by Lear and his roughnecks made things that much sweeter. It was a time for the East and West to forget the past, cover up old wounds and to give the West equal say with the Eastern Big Four in a joint operation.

None of this was in the mind of Lear in the frantic hours after the game. Wearing only a ten-gallon hat and chewing on an unlighted cigar, he rumbled up and down his Royal York Hotel room listening to the hollering of Calgary fans on the streets below. In his book, emotions were for little old ladies. "Listen to 'em, will yeh?" he asked. "I'm a big hero now, but wait until next year when we lose a few."

All the while, though, he had a grin on his face. He loved it — and it was nice to be a winner. He didn't realize that he had played a role in shaping the greatest revolution in Canadian sports history that sunny afternoon. He knew only that "my kids came through for me" and, in the weeks ahead, when Calgary was still hung over, he would get down to cases with his bosses and go for a long-term contract. Before the year was out he had a new five-year pact.

Things started to move. While officials East and West were counting their blessings for those wonderful Alberta fans, Alderman MacKay and Lear, the Toronto Junior Board of Trade hopped on the bandwagon. Its members started the organization of pre-game festivities. They stuck to the Calgary script, added a few refinements here and there with Miss Grey Cup beauty contests, parties, dances.

Grey Cup finals became automatic sellouts. Seat prices were scaled up to a top of $1.50 in 1948 and gate receipts that year totalled $26,655, a figure that would pay about one-third of the cost of staging the final in the 1960s.

New stadiums were built, others enlarged. The 1954 British Empire Games provided Vancouver with the largest stadium in the country. The British Columbia Lions were admitted into the WIFU that year and in 1955 the largest crowd in the history of organized team sports in Canada — 39,417 — packed Empire Stadium for the Cup final. Gate receipts totalled $197,182.91, more than 100 times the revenue of that ill-fated 1940 Ottawa-Toronto Balmy Beach final.

The mating of television with football in 1952 brought league, play-off games, the Cup festivities and the final itself into the country's living rooms. Plus, of course, more football fans and ready cash for

Canadian teams. Big money was there for the picking by American players and coaches and, eventually, for Canadian super-stars such as Ottawa's Russ Jackson who signed a 1969 contract for a reported $37,000 plus bonuses; or Terry Evanshen who signed a three-year pact with Montreal Alouettes in 1970 for a reported $100,000-plus.

Canadian coaches flocked to U.S. bowl games and congregated around the goalposts to woo players enroute to dressing rooms. National Football League clubs in the U.S. hollered foul. Lawsuits followed. NFL salaries were forced up in the bidding for talent with the Canadians and, finally, the bidding slowed down with the birth in 1960 of the American Football League. The Canadians, with a few exceptions, were shut out in the costly NFL-AFL battle for players.

The Big Four and WIFU leagues started working as a unit. The aim was to trim the voting powers of the ORFU, the Intercollegiate Union, the Quebec Rugby Football Union and, eventually, the Maritimes Football Union in the CRU. And, naturally, to gain possession of the Grey Cup. The ORFU found itself in a squeeze play by the bigger and richer unions to gain voting control of the CRU. The idea was to kick the ORFU out of Cup competition.

The ORFU, born in 1873 and with seven Cup winners in 14 challenges, resisted the move. Meetings became explosive, but nothing could stop the ouster. The big leagues eventually gained voting control of the CRU in 1953 and formed the Canadian Football Council. This stopped the ludicrous situation whereby minor leagues had a say in the Big Four-WIFU playing rules, import regulations, the scores of other league matters and the operation of the Cup final.

In 1955, schedules were arranged by the Big Four and WIFU which would not allow time for an ORFU cup challenge. Three years later, the Canadian Football League was formed and Syd Halter was appointed commissioner. On June 7, 1966, the CRU handed the Grey Cup trophy over to the CFL and six months later the CRU disbanded, to be reborn as the Canadian Amateur Football Association. Thus, 45 years after the CRU took the advice of an anonymous letter writer in 1921 and arranged East-West meetings for a $48 hunk of metal originally donated for the Canadian amateur championship, the pros had owned it. And the clumsy oafs had it stolen.

On Dec. 20, 1969, it was stolen from its showcase at Lansdowne Park in Ottawa, home of the Rough Riders. Police, acting on a tip, recovered it intact in a locker in the Royal York Hotel in Toronto on Feb. 16, 1970.

The Canadian Football League didn't appear to be disturbed about the theft in 1969. Jake Gaudaur, appointed commissioner in 1968, cleared up the CFL's apparent indifferent attitude in May, 1970. "We didn't have to worry about it," he said. "An informer told the police he knew who had taken it from Lansdowne Park. He also told police where the Cup was located. We knew it was just a matter of time until it showed up."

Shortly after the Cup's disappearance football fans were chuckling about the theft. Nothing like that had ever happened while the CRU had the trophy, they said, except for that 1966 evening in Hamilton when an exhuberant fan borrowed it overnight. But the much-maligned Union had enough troubles through the years without someone running off with the only tangible thing it possessed. Look back to the explosive years when the CRU dropped the West from Cup competition; when it stubbornly resisted suggestions from the West about rule changes that would open up the game, and when it was criticized for what fans called faulty Cup ticket distribution.

All of this, though, is just a part of the Grey Cup story and of football in Canada. There is the all-important human element, the men who played away back when, and who built up life-long friendships with men they played with and against. These men have stored up fond memories of those days when they played with or without helmets or without the sophisticated armor such as face guards of a later era.

And how about the fellow who started the Grey Cup in 1909? Earl Grey never did see a Cup final. He returned to his ancestral home in England in 1911, not knowing really whether he had come up with a winner or whether the final would develop into an East-West annual playoff as he intended it to be.

The trophy? It arrived on the scene in March, 1910, a bit late due to the Earl's forgetfulness since University of Toronto Blues had won the title on Dec. 4, 1909.

On hindsight, and considering the Cup's career, that little oversight was an appropriate touch.

CHAPTER II

THE WILD YEARS

1909-1915

The action was spirited on and off the field, setting the pattern in many ways for what was to come: the wild, untamed years when football costs roared out of sight, clubs lost money and officials were blasted for faulty Cup ticket distribution.

Club budgets were frugal and 60 cents for bandages was no little expenditure. Playing rules were strict. Scalpers made a killing. Inter-city rivalry was intense. Spectators were colorful, noisy and daring. Players were tough and roisterous. Fans flocked to games by railway, boat, tally-ho, carriages, and the high, open motor cars of the day. Stadiums were enlarged or built to accommodate the crowds which sometimes failed to materialize.

This was the picture of the 1909-1915 era that produced great players who continued their love of the game either as club or league officials or as spectators. And men who became prominent in many fields. There was Dr. Smirle Lawson, the original Big Train of Canadian football and later Ontario's chief coroner from 1937 to 1951. Another was Frank (King) Clancy, father of an illustrious son who gained national fame with the old Ottawa Senators and Toronto Maple Leafs of the National Hockey League.

Another was Jim McCann, later minister of national revenue in the Liberal governments of Mackenzie King and Louis St. Laurent. He started his practice in Hamilton as a 24-year-old graduate of medicine from Queen's University and immediately caught a place with the Tigers of 1911-1912, with such greats as George Awrey, Art Moore, Frank (Dutch) Burton, Sam Manson, Bob (Izzy) Isbister. Dr. McCann died in 1961 at the age of 74.

Gene Lockhart, later to gain international fame as an actor, was a benchwarmer on the 1911 Toronto Argonaut club. Another great was Hughie Gall, who could kick a ball 70 yards with either foot and who wore his baseball shoes on the football field. He simply substituted cleats for spikes. There was hulky, hard-hitting Ross (Husky) Craig, fore-runner to another Hamilton hardrock, Brian Timmis. Glad Murphy, Hal DeGruchy, Jack O'Connor, Ben Simpson, Bull Ritchie, Billy Foulds, Alex Sinclair; to the swinging generation, these are only names of a distant past.

Following them were other Canadian-born players whose names became familiar to sports enthusiasts across the country: Russ Jackson, Normie Kwong, Jeff Russel, Ernie Cox, Bunny Wadsworth, Lionel Conacher, Joe Krol, Ches McCance, Les Lear, Royal Copeland, Dave Sprague, Eddie Emmerson, Norm Perry, Tiny Hermann, George Fraser, Eddie (Dynamite) James and his son, Gerry, Lou Mogul, Ron Stewart, Jeff Nicklin, Art West, Lou (Rosy) Adelman, Bill Boivin, Bobby Simpson, Ted Reeve, Bobby Porter, Harry (Red) Foster, Jack Wedley, Bill Zock, Seymour Wilson, Cliff Roseborough, Jimmy Simpson.

Many of the players in the 1909 era bought their own uniforms — shoes, canvas pants with pads sewn in, stockings, canvas jackets with a little bit of padding around the shoulders. They played when it was a five-minute penalty for rough play or for talking back to game officials. Substitutions were allowed in case of injury in the first half, but no substitution was allowed in the second for any cause in 1909.

In 1915, subs were allowed during any quarter of the game in the case of injuries but a player, once removed, could not return to the game except with the consent of the team captains. It was 14-man-a-side football until 1921 when they switched to the present-day 12. Maybe they received a cap or some other inexpensive memento as a member of a Cup-winning team. They celebrated by munching sandwiches and drinking pop in the dressing room or, as one team's financial statement showed, "special water" that cost 70 cents, plus "liquid refreshment" that cost $1.75. One could only guess about that.

Some Cup final teams made money, others just managed to finish the season in the black or, maybe, lose a few dollars. This sort of thing happened years later. In 1929, the books after the Regina-Hamilton game showed a loss on the day of $13.92, not counting Regina's expenses of getting to Hamilton and back home.

In the 1950s, when clubs were operating on budgets of $400,000 and $500,000 a year, some Cup winners found that success on the field

21

was not matched in the financial returns. They lost money on the season.

Fans passed up some Cup games in the early years when they figured the contest would be a pushover for one club. The same situation existed in the 1920s, 1930s and early 1940s. At the other end of the scale, there weren't enough tickets to accommodate the fans who wanted to watch the season's-end game and the Canadian Rugby Union was blamed. Again, it was a fore-runner to those hectic, ticket-seeking days after 1948.

Earl Grey must have wondered what sort of hanky-panky was going on in Toronto in 1909. Strange things were happening just months after he donated the $48 trophy. The Toronto daily newspapers billed the Ottawa-University of Toronto game at Rosedale Field as the "Dominion Championship". But surely someone had erred. This game was only the Cup semi-final with the winner to meet Toronto Parkdale, Ontario Rugby Football Union champion, for the trophy.

The "Dominion Championship" game would, of course, put the ORFU club out in the cold which, certainly, was not Earl Grey's intention. Many years later, in the early 1950s, the newly-formed Canadian Football League booted the ORFU out of Cup contention and ORFU historians acidly pointed out that the Union had been down-graded from the Cup's inception.

But, in 1909, the Dominion championship billing was just a play on words. The Toronto newspapers, and football enthusiasts, felt that this Ottawa-Varsity game, scheduled for Nov. 27, was the big one, that the green and white ORFU Parkdales would be patsies against the winner in the final on Dec. 4.

The Riders, coached by King Clancy, had whipped through Big Four opposition and Varsity had little trouble in college play. The pre-game ballyhoo resulted in fans lining up before the box office 24 hours ahead of the kickoff. Marathon dances were held throughout the night to pass the time and before the sun was up on Saturday thousands had gathered outside Rosedale Field.

The crush was so terrific when the gates opened that the start was delayed 30 minutes. Rosedale was built to accommodate about 3,400 persons and an estimated 12,000 stampeded into the grounds, sitting 15 deep around the playing field in front of open carriages occupied by raccoon-coated, top-hatted gentlemen and their ladies.

Seat prices ranged from 25 cents to $1.25 and the elite happily paid a dollar a carriage and 50 cents an occupant to get into the grounds.

The game almost didn't come off. Early in the week Ottawa players claimed that the club executive had gobbled up the team's ticket quota and they threatened to strike. Officials relented 48 hours before the kickoff and harmony was restored. This 1909 semi-final was no contest. The collegians, coached by Harry Griffith, the grand old man of Canadian football who retired in 1949 after a 50-year career, won 31-7. In the excitement, some fans almost tumbled out of their seats on poles, rooftops of nearby buildings, and trees surrounding the field.

A week later, and again at Rosedale Field, Varsity met Parkdale. The crowd of 3,800 contributed $2,616.40 in gate receipts and Varsity won easily, 26-6. Hughie Gall, who later was to lose his life while serving with the Canadian Army overseas in the First World War, kicked eight singles — a Cup record that still stands — and also scored a touchdown for a 13-point afternoon.

The 1910 final, played Nov. 26 at the old Cricket Grounds in Hamilton, marked the beginning of the boisterous revelry surrounding the Cup. University of Toronto Blues and Hamilton Tigers were the principals in the contest and Toronto supporters, almost 5,000 of them, travelled the 40 miles by special trains, boats, tally-ho and car. They arrived in Hamilton hours before the kickoff, roamed the downtown streets and taunted Tiger fans in their yellow and black colors. Police patrolled the area between the factions and arranged that they march to the stadium separately.

An hour before the kickoff crowds rushed the ticket wickets. About 700 paid the 50-cent standing-room charge, another 2,000 broke down the fences, clambered onto the scoreboard and stadium roof and dared police to get them down.

The collegians won 16-7 on a field of mud following an early-morning rain, on a touchdown and two singles by Reddy Dixon, a touchdown, convert and single by Jack Maynard and two singles by Hughie Gall. When the news of Varsity's win spread to downtown Hamilton, store owners bolted their doors and sent employees home. Hundreds of Toronto and Hamilton fans roamed the streets until nearly midnight spoiling for a fight. Things appeared to be getting out of control and excited citizens called the police. Hamilton's deputy police chief arrived on the scene, climbed atop a paddy wagon and told the mob to make as much noise as it pleased but that the city jail would accommodate trouble-makers. He was cheered and the trouble was averted.

Ticket scalpers did a big business in the days preceding that game. They got as much as $100 for four $1.50 seats and on the day of the contest 50-cent bleacher seats sold for $3.50 and $1 reserved seats for $10. Secret workouts, which became a way of life in later years, were held by the Tigers in the six days before the game and police were hired to shoo away would-be spies. In breaks during the game Varsity students carrying heavy wire brushes dashed onto the field to remove mud from the collegians' shoes.

Before the Nov. 25 final rolled around at Toronto between University of Toronto and Toronto Argonauts in 1911, Earl Grey had returned to his home at Howick Hall, Alnwick, Northumberland, not knowing that Calgary Tigers, Western Canada Rugby League winners, had notified the CRU that they would like to take a crack at the Eastern champs.

The challenge arrived too late. The CRU had made plans for the Varsity-Argo clash. And just 90 minutes before the kickoff the last nail was driven into the University of Toronto's new Varsity Stadium, the midtown bowl that was to be the scene of many memorable Cup clashes in the next 43 years. University officials left nothing to chance. In constant touch with the Toronto weather bureau, they received word four days before the game that a snowstorm might hit the city.

They were ready with their version of a tarpaulin. Six tons of straw were piled onto the field the following day and on Friday, Nov. 24, it snowed. Let it come, said organizers, the straw was an effective shield. They were wrong. The snow penetrated the covering and when the straw was lifted on game day the field was frozen and the footing was treacherous. Students soaked up what little moisture was left in depressions on the ground but this did little good.

A crowd of 13,687, the largest to witness a football game in the country to that date, saw the game and newspapers complained the stadium was "quite too small for a fixture of such importance." The collegians, favored at 2-to-1 odds, won 14-7, their third consecutive Cup triumph. Frank Knight and Allan Ramsay scored Varsity touchdowns, known then as a "try" and Jack Maynard kicked the "goals from try" — converts — and a single. Smirle Lawson added a single. Argonaut scoring was handled by Ross Binkley who kicked four singles and a placement, known in these days as a "goal from the field."

The CRU allowed the clubs to handle the ticket sale, and this practice was criticized. Season subscribers had first call and only 500 bleacher seats, at a dollar a throw, were available to the general public. Scalpers — and Argos — made a killing. The Big Four club's share from the $14,233 receipts was $6,002, a sum that could keep amateur clubs operating for years.

Hamilton Alerts became the first ORFU club to win the Cup with an 11-4 victory in 1912 over the 5-to-1 favored Argos at Hamilton and, as happened to other ORFU Cup finalists in the future, there was an ironic twist. First, the Alerts never did get the trophy because of Varsity's decision that anyone who wanted it had to beat the college club. The Cup remained in the U of T showcase. Also, fan interest was low. The experts figured it would be a soft touch for Argos and only 5,337 persons turned up at the Cricket Field. This game almost didn't start for probably the most unusual reason in Canadian football history.

There wasn't a ball in sight just before the teams were ready to take the field. Eventually, one person kicked in a dressing-room door and retrieved the only football available. The man in charge of the football had inadvertently locked it inside and had vanished with the key. It cost the CRU $1.75 to replace the door.

The game finally got underway, nearly an hour after the advertised kickoff, and a couple of hours later Argonaut players were wishing that the man had taken the ball with him. Argos made yards only twice. Ross (Husky) Craig scored a touchdown and kicked the convert for the Alerts and Norm (Tout) Leckie booted five singles. Alerts conceded a safety touch and Crossen Clarke kicked two Argo singles. McGill Redmen from Montreal had won the college title. The players held an off-the-field huddle and decided to pass up further play because they couldn't afford the time away from their studies.

Toronto Parkdale was back again in 1913 and, once again, an ORFU standard-bearer laid an egg at the box-office. Only 2,100 fans were on hand at Hamilton where the Tigers mauled the Toronto club 44-2.

Husky Craig scored 15 points on three touchdowns, a single-game record that was tied in 1921 by Lionel Conacher and in 1938 by Red Storey, both of Argonauts. This mark was eventually to be eclipsed by two players — Jackie Parker of Edmonton in 1956 who scored 19 points and Jimmy Van Pelt of Winnipeg Blue Bombers who scored 22 in 1958.

University of Toronto at last unlocked its trophy showcase and surrendered the Cup to Toronto Argonauts in 1914. On Dec. 5 at Varsity Stadium and with more than 10,000 fans in attendance, Argos made it 14-2 over the collegians on touchdowns by Glad Murphy and Freddie Mills, a convert and a placement by Jack O'Connor. O'Connor, later club president, made Cup history when he attempted seven field goals and was good on only one.

The 1915 final was the same old story for ORFU clubs. The Varsity Stadium field was greasy, only 2,868 fans turned out and they produced the second smallest gate receipts for a Cup game — $1,887.50. Disappointed supporters of the Toronto Rowing and Athletic Association club from the ORFU showed their displeasure at Hamilton Tigers' 13-7 victory in a most unusual manner. They staged the only on-field near-riot in the Cup's history.

At the final whistle, someone in the bleachers shouted "Get Dixon," signalling a stampede from the stands in the direction of Referee Reddy (Ewart) Dixon who ran to safety under the stands and into the Toronto dressing room.

The fans were riled at some of his calls and they milled around the field and in the area of the dressing rooms for minutes until they decided that Dixon, a former Varsity player, wasn't going to show until the stadium was cleared. The game itself developed into a kicking duel and each club punted 36 times, a Cup record. Each team received $583.70 as its share of the gate and, with the First World War on and football suspended for the duration, the teams donated the money to patriotic funds.

Many of the players switched to khaki uniforms but before going overseas Tiger players took the trophy to a silversmith in Hamilton and had him record their 1908 Canadian championship victory over the University of Toronto on the Cup. Their wild scheme had Cup historians puzzled for years. In 1951, when the CRU decided to enlarge the trophy to make room for new names officials took due notice of the inaccuracy but went along with the gag. They decided to let it stay rather than erase an interesting item from the Cup story.

The young 60-minute men of the early years certainly didn't make any money out of their chosen sport but they provided a lot of excitement.

26

CHAPTER III

THE CHANGING STYLES

The Twenties

The Roaring Twenties. Bathtub gin. Speakeasies. Clip joints. Wacky dances. The Charleston. The Black Bottom. Raccoon coats. Oil-slick hair parted dead centre. Yes, sir, you were the life of the party if you could keep time to a catchy little tune called The Varsity Drag on a washboard.

The First World War had ended and those who had made it back home had a lot of catching up to do. And money in their pockets to do it with. Live it up. There's no tomorrow. Let's have a party. Pile into the roadsters, snuggle up to your flappers in the rumble seat and head for the honky-tonk highway spots.

Football was on the move again. Teams started rebuilding. Grease the gates and let the mobs pour through. Many of the fine young Canadians who had changed to khaki from football uniforms had returned and were putting the pads on again.

Significant changes in the Grey Cup's history were taking place. The trophy itself appeared on the scene in 1920 after being deposited in a vault — and forgotten — during the war years by a Cup trustee. Trustees handed it over to the Canadian Rugby Union — a move that was to give the Union innumerable pains and troubles.

In 1921, the West made its first challenge. This, undoubtedly, was the turning point in Canadian football history. The East made it clear that it couldn't care less about the Western challenges, and the West reciprocated. Western clubs didn't bother to challenge the East on three occasions — in 1924, 1926 and 1927. There was internal squabbling in the West and the teams were also fed up waiting for the East to declare its champion. They packed their equipment and called it a year.

The Twenties also marked the last time college teams played in the

Cup final. In 1926, the University of Toronto Blues met Ottawa for the Cup. They lost 10-7. College clubs continued to make their bids but they couldn't get past the Eastern semi-finals and, in 1937, the Intercollegiate Union quietly dropped out of contention.

In the Twenties, football fans beat a steady path to the stadiums on Saturday afternoons — until Grey Cup Day, that is. Maybe it was because of the appearance of the weak Western champions in the final. Maybe it was the fact that throughout this decade Cup Day weather was horrible — rain, cold, snow, freezing temperatures, biting cold winds. More to the point, Eastern football fans may have objected to the intrusion of the West in what had hitherto been an all-Eastern show. Whatever the reason, these early East-West finals were dreadful flops at the gate.

Only twice in the decade did the attendance reach five figures and, pointedly, it was an all-Eastern final on each occasion — 10,088 in 1920 for a Toronto Varsity-Toronto Argonaut meeting, and 13,676 in 1927 when Toronto Balmy Beach met Hamilton Tigers. In other years, attendance varied from 9,558 in 1921 when Edmonton Eskimos became the first Westerners to challenge, and lost to Argonauts, to 1,906 in 1929 for a Regina-Hamilton contest. Tigers won.

The West made six trips East and scored a total of only five points. Hardly impressive, but to the more sophisticated Eastern football analysts, the West was slowly getting to the point when it would some day — soon — beat the East.

The Twenties opened with a natural box-office attraction — Toronto Argonauts of the Big Four versus University of Toronto, coached by the one-time great, Laddie Cassels. They had met twice before in the Cup, each winning once — Varsity in 1911 and Argos in 1914. Argonaut coaching chores were split between Mike Rodden and Sinc McEvenue. In Rodden, they had a hard-bitten and colorful leader of varied talents. A former star at Queen's University in Kingston, Rodden eventually coached football teams to 27 titles during a busy career. As a hockey referee, he was to become a member of the National Hockey League Hall of Fame. He coached a couple of Grey Cup winners and held the job of sports editor with the old Toronto Globe.

In 1920 he and McEvenue had lots of power in such legendary figures as Harry Batstone, who later was to gain national fame as a member of Cup-winning Queen's teams, Jack O'Connor, Alex Sin-

28

clair, Alex Romeril, Cap Fear, Glad Murphy, Shrimp Cochrane, Frank Wright, Glenn Sullivan, Walter Gilhooley, Bobby Polson, Gord Britnell. Captain was Joe Breen who, years later, was to become well known in Canadian financial circles as head of Canada Cement. Punter was Dunc Munro, later an Ottawa Senator and Montreal Maroon star in the NHL.

The Blues also had their share of greats and fans decided that adverse weather conditions wouldn't steer them clear of Varsity Stadium on Saturday, Dec. 4. Rain started to fall the morning of the game and continued until just 30 minutes before the kickoff. Despite the slippery going, they saw a dandy. Varsity won 16-3 on touchdowns by Warren Snyder, Jo-Jo Stirrett and Red Mackenzie, who also kicked one convert. Munro, making his only appearance in a Cup final, scored the Argo points — singles in each of the first, third and fourth quarters.

Varsity then disappeared from the Cup scene for five years while Queen's, with the Harry Batstone-Pep Leadlay duo on the roster, provided the college opposition. At last, in 1921, a truly national East-West final became a reality. With it, came Lionel Pretoria Conacher who later was to be named Canada's outstanding football player and all-round athlete of the half-century in the 1950 Canadian Press poll. Billy Foulds, CRU president, had heeded the advice of an anonymous letter writer to get going on a national championship. He set up a meeting with Moe Lieberman, manager of the Western champion Edmonton Eskimos. Moe's financial terms were somewhat overwhelming.

He wanted a guarantee of $4,000 if the East insisted that the 1921 final be played in its back yard. Foulds, who had quarterbacked Cup-winning University of Toronto clubs in 1909 and 1910, eventually agreed. Years later, shortly before his death in 1953, he recalled the circumstances. "The Eskimos wanted $4,000 and the CRU didn't have four thousand cents in the kitty. We scrounged around, got the money somehow and that is how the East-West final started." He didn't explain that he had personally guaranteed the $4,000. Associates disclosed this after his death.

With the money assured, the Eskimos, staffed by American college players who knew little of the Canadian game, took a train for Toronto. To Western fans, it was unfortunate the Eskimos picked a year when the Eastern champs were loaded with high-class talent.

29

Conacher joined Batstone in the Argo backfield. It was Lionel's only appearance in a Cup final and the Eskimos and 9,558 fans who paid $9,991.30 to see the game, probably never forgot it. Distinctive in his peaked cap, he scored two touchdowns, kicked a field goal and two singles in the 23-0 victory. And he played only the first three quarters. He and team-mate Alex Romeril had an appointment on the ice a few hours later and, with the score 21-0, they left the stadium. Conacher, a bruising defenceman, played 60 minutes that night but his Toronto Aura Lee club lost 4-2 to Romeril's Toronto Granites.

Conacher's 15-point afternoon matched the single-game Cup record established by Husky Craig of the 1913 Hamilton Tigers.

Lionel, who later played on two Stanley Cup Championship teams — Chicago Black Hawks in 1934 and Montreal Maroons in 1935 — died suddenly in 1954 in Ottawa during a Commons-Press Gallery baseball game.

The Eskimos were no pushovers despite the shutout. Coached by Deacon White, the roster included Jazz Moore, George Day, Vic Yancey, Miles Palmer, Clare Darling, Ab Emery, Art Creighton, Curly Lorman, Doc Dunsworth, Russ (Bullet) Burnett, Billy Rankin, Blossom Seeley, Doc Murdoch, Jim Enright, George Shieman, Howard Harrison, Noble Stevens, Bill Fowler, Jack Fraser and Red McGill. Eastern critics said they "amazed fans with battering line drives" but had nothing to stop the wild running through the snowflurries of Conacher and Batstone.

Then came Queen's and the start of an era. The Tricolor, anchored by Leadlay and Batstone, was to dominate the football scene from 1922 and 1924. The university was serious about winning football games. Leadlay had been acquired from Hamilton Tigers and Batstone, who hadn't completed his matriculation, suddenly left the Cup champion Argonauts to go to college. The fact that a matriculation was an entrance requirement didn't seem to apply to football players. And Batstone proved to be as good with books as he was on a football field. He hadn't taken Latin at high school and needed it for his university course. In four months, during part of which he also played football, he crammed himself with enough Latin to pass the Christmas examinations.

He went on to graduate from medical school and emerged from Queen's as a respected doctor with a practice in Kingston. Only 4,700 persons turned up in Kingston in 1922 to watch Edmonton, this time

30

called the Elks, meet the classy college kids. The Tricolor won 13-1 and it was a Batstone-Leadlay innovation that led to the West's downfall. The Elks were befuddled by their antics as the two passed the ball like a basketball over their opponents' heads. This probably was the start of the hot-potato end run. In later years, particularly in the 1930s some coaches tried it, liked it and claimed they had started something new.

Edmonton had arrived with a few tricks of its own. One was the art of grabbing an opponent's sleeve and giving a yank. The strategy was that a ball carrier who could be swung in circles in this manner was forced to slow down, making him an easy target for the tacklers. However, favored Queen's was too elusive and Edmonton, balked on defence, didn't have much to fall back on. The Elks managed only six first downs. They went home with a world of respect for the football-playing ability of Queen's. Despite the small crowd turnout, interest on the part of the players was high. "We were serious in those days," said Leadlay years after his retirement. "We recognized the Grey Cup as the Canadian championship. That was every football player's aim. It was the apex. Well, let's say it was the pinnacle."

Maybe it was to Eastern players, but the Westerners took an altogether different attitude in the coming years. Crossing the country, it seemed in 1923, took a great deal of planning and compromise. Team officials didn't merely announce that all players were to report at a specific time of departure. Nor did they spell out orders on a dressing-room blackboard. In Regina, everybody got into the act and it almost resulted in the Roughriders not making the trip East. Players and team officials had definite views on the subject.

A serious internal issue developed. Players wanted to travel to Toronto via one rail route, team management by another. The players issued an ultimatum: Go our way or we don't go at all. High-handed? Could be, but remember that football was strictly amateur according to the Amateur Athletic Union of Canada rules and players undoubtedly figured they should have some say in the operation. After several meetings, the two factions reached agreement and started the long trip East. It might have been better if they had been unable to iron out their differences and stayed home. Roughriders lost 54-0, the worst beating suffered by a team in the annual classic.

Whatever the reason for their humiliating defeat, there was no disagreement on the routing of the return trip. It was unanimous:

the shortest and fastest route to Regina. And to kill time on the way, they could read accounts of the game in the newspapers—and sizzle. "A farcical final," was one comment. They had been up against a superlative team, coached by Billy Hughes. Queen's had been undefeated all season, had outscored the opposition 70-14 and had allowed only one touchdown.

They dazzled the Roughriders and rewrote most of the record book at their expense. The incomparable Pep Leadlay kicked a record seven converts and added two singles before a crowd of 8,629 at Varsity Stadium who paid $8,746.65 to watch the massacre. It was to be five years before Regina recovered sufficiently to win the Western title again. Some never made another trip East as players—via any railroad.

Nothing could have stopped Queen's. The field was excellent—the last time in the decade that the weatherman was kind on Cup Day—and the bitterly-disappointed Roughriders took their lumps in 43-degree weather under slightly overcast skies. Years later, Rider players loved to tell how tough they were. It was customary before a game for each lineman to put a dollar in the hat, the proceeds going to the first man to draw blood from an opponent. It was customary, too, for each lineman to plant his fist in the face of his opposite number on the last play of the game. This, of course, resulted in some merry free-for-alls that were worth the price of admission.

But there were no bloody faces in Queen's dressing room. The red faces, this time, belonged to the Regina players.

In 1924, the question in the East was how Winnipeg Victorias might have made out in the Cup final. No one will ever know. The Western club was so busy fighting about the proposed trip East the players never did get around to making it. It was the same old story—which railway route to take—and they were stubborn about it. The players finally decided to go without management and on the railroad of their choice. "Go ahead," officials said, "but we won't allow you to use the team name." Meetings were held. Finally, the club wrote the CRU to say they were ready. Too late, said the CRU. Queen's which had beaten Toronto Balmy Beach 11-3 at Varsity Stadium in Toronto on Nov. 29, had packed its gear and the players were out of training.

The CRU awarded Queen's the Cup and Billy Hughes became the first coach in Cup history to win three straight—a feat matched only twice in later years. Teddy Morris did it with Toronto Argonauts in 1945-6-7 and Pop Ivy with Edmonton Eskimos in 1954-5-6. The

Beaches, coached by Mike Rodden, weren't supposed to give Queen's much of a game. The college's scrub team had beaten Beaches 32-0 in an exhibition game earlier in the year but the surprising ORFU club outplayed the first-string Tricolor for most of the Cup contest.

It was Beaches' first appearance in a Cup final and the game seemed to set a precedent for the luckless Toronto club. Only 5,978 persons were in the stands, the field was muddy, the skies overcast, and it was cold. Balmy Beach was "that other club" in Toronto. Fans supported Argonauts in the Big Four and University of Toronto in the college group while Beaches played in semi-privacy. That year marked the last Cup appearance of Queen's. The college played in Eastern semi-finals another four times, in 1925, 1927, 1929 and 1930, but lost each time to the Big Four titleholder. It went out with a fine record—three for three.

Winnipeg Victorias? Well, they quietly faded away. The team even changed its name. Winnipeg discarded the distasteful Victorias tag after the bickering of 1924 and in 1925 Winnipeg Tammany Tigers went to Ottawa, lost 24-1 to the Senators on a muddy field. The ridicule and abuse they received from the Eastern critics for their Cup efforts lit the fuse of long-smouldering hatred. Critics said these fiascos must be stopped. Back in friendly Winnipeg, players and team officials were infuriated when they heard that they had been classed as inter-mediates. Tigers were also told that the 6,900 fans had paid only $6,000 in gate receipts—and that their share wasn't enough to pay expenses.

It was the first East-West final that proved to be a losing proposition at the box-office. The panning from the "experts" wasn't a true summing up of the situation, considering the almost-impossible playing conditions. Lansdowne Park was a large puddle of water. The players slipped and skittered on a horrible, muddy field and the Westerners weren't exactly accustomed to such slop. It had rained heavily the night before the game and throughout the morning. The downpour stopped shortly before the kickoff.

The Tammany Tigers had been considered by some Western observers as the best team the West had sent East in search of the Cup and it was unfortunate the field was in such a mess. They were coached by Harold Roth and the roster included such players as Clair Warner, Dick Buckingham, Lyman van Vliet, Johnny Laing, Art Shaw, Ward McVey, Bert Binney, Oliver Redpath, Eddie Grant, Cam Counsell,

Sonny Coultry, Jack Milledge, Jack McMahon, Harry Bullock and Lou (Rosy) Adelman.

On the Ottawa team was the Iron Man of Canadian senior football— Eddie Emmerson. He tried out with the club in 1909, when J. A. D. McCurdy got the Silver Dart into the air for the first time, and he didn't quit until 1937 when Canada had a coast-to-coast airline. Emmerson made the team in 1912 and played 25 full seasons, 24 of them as a flying wing—later called a flanker—and one as a snap, later known as a centre. He died early in 1970.

Charlie Connell scored two Senator touchdowns. Edgar Mulrooney and Don Young each scored one and Charlie Lynch kicked four singles. Eddie Grant kicked Tammany Tigers' lone point in the third quarter. Remember the name, because Eddie later became a game official and figured in a highly-controversial game against Winnipeg in the late 1930s.

Again, in 1926, the West decided to sit out the final. The champion Regina Roughriders were riled enough at the treatment given Tammany Tigers to go East and rattle a few bones, but they were fed up with the dictatorial attitude of the Easterners. Roughriders had finished their games early in November and they weren't enchanted with the idea of loafing while the East conducted its playoffs among the Big Four, ORFU and college champions. They called it quits.

The Cup final was scheduled for Dec. 4 at Toronto and it brought together Ottawa Senators, the defending champions, and University of Toronto. Ottawa won 10-7 in bitterly-cold weather conditions that would have been ideal for Regina Roughriders who were used to tough Prairie winters. The official ticket sale was 8,276 but only 4,000 hardy souls were in the stands. Hundreds of numbed fans paid admission fees, started for their seats and quickly changed their minds and headed for the ticket sellers to get their money back.

Most of them never made it. Others were coming in while still hundreds of others congregated under the stands in their coonskin coats. The confusion was so great the reluctant ticket-holders were unable to get refunds. That's how it was that early December Saturday afternoon at Varsity Stadium with a teeth-chattering wind whipping across the open spaces. An inch of snow had fallen the night before and the field was a patchwork of ice and snow. Temperatures were zero.

That was the year the college union dropped out of contention.

In 1926, the Ottawa Senators almost didn't make it to the final against Varsity. They met Toronto Balmy Beach in the semi-final and trailed 6-1 at the half. Ottawa's Joe Miller was the hero. He kicked six singles. In the final his clutch punting gave Senators their 10-7 margin of victory. But that was the end of Miller's football career. The same night he joined New York Americans of the National Hockey League as a goalkeeper. Two years later he was back in a championship game, in the memorable Stanley Cup final in which grey-haired 44-year-old Lester Patrick, manager of the Rangers, stepped in as a replacement for Lorne Chabot, his injured goalkeeper.

Rangers beat Montreal Maroons 2-1 in overtime and Patrick picked up Miller from the Americans for the remainder of the series. He gave up only three goals in two games and Rangers won the best-of-five series 3-2. It was the last time Miller's name hit the headlines. He died at his home in Toronto on July 31, 1963.

In 1927, Toronto Balmy Beach made the Cup final again, but this time they won, a tremendous 9-6 victory over Hamilton Tigers on Nov. 26, at Toronto Varsity Stadium. This was an all-Eastern final because Regina Roughriders won the Western title and decided to pass up the trip East for the second straight year and for the same reason: Why wait idly until the East was ready?

The Beaches, even in their few periods of glory, ranked as a throwback to an earlier era in Canadian football, when the game's main object was the enjoyment of the players. They were happy if they attracted enough customers to finance the post-game festivities. More often than not, their share of the gate receipts didn't go much farther. And when Regina Roughriders decided to stay home that year, sophisticated supporters of Tigers saw no valid reason why the name of the Big Four champions couldn't be scratched on the Cup without the formality of an all-Eastern final. Toronto sports writers agreed and one dismissed the game as "a nuisance that can't be avoided."

Furthermore, the Toronto east-enders lived up to their reputation of invariably getting the worst possible weather for their most important games. The rain started at noon and kept up until half-time, leaving the field mud-splattered and making the footing treacherous.

But there were early indications that the breaks might favor the Ontario Rugby Football Union champions. In spite of the gloomy pre-game forecasts and the gloomier weather, the crowd numbered 13,676, just 11 short of the record set in 1911, the first year the final was played in the new Varsity Stadium. Beaches weren't overwhelmed by the capacity house. The players undoubtedly made a mental note of the handsome contribution the paying fans would make towards their winter-long parties.

It soon became evident that the Beaches, accustomed to playing in slop, were far more at home than the Tabbies. And spectators saw quite a football game. The first thing that went wrong with the pre-game script was that Beaches quarterback Alex Ponton, later to become the Beaches' coach, blocked a return kick that enabled Ernie Crowhurst to kick a single. Minutes later, Ted Reeve led the hard-charging Beach line in another assault and another Hamilton kick was blocked by Ike Commins. This time, the ball bounced into the hands of Bobby Reid, a young inside wing. Nobody laid a hand on him all the way to the Tiger end zone and Beaches finished the first quarter with a 6-0 lead.

Yip Foster, a tremendous punter rated in the same class with Lionel Conacher, stretched it to 9-0 with three singles in the second quarter. Tigers, still very much alive but with their pride wounded, came out strong in the second half. Pep Leadlay, the old Toronto Argonaut and Queen's University halfback, scored a single. Then he shot an onside kick to Tebor McKelvey who raced for a touchdown. Led by Brian Timmis, Tigers continued to push their lighter opponents around, picking up 17 first downs over-all to Beaches' three. But they couldn't make it pay off. Late in the game, Red Moore pulled Beaches out of a hole when he took a punt behind his own goal-line and slipped and slithered to his 30-yard line.

Beaches were to surmount the odds a second time to win the Cup in 1930. After that, there was a long, slow period of decline. They finally folded after the 1958 season when they lost all 12 of their ORFU starts and failed to make enough money to pay for their uniforms. Other football teams have had more talent, more luck and bigger bank accounts. But ask any graduate of the roistering east-enders and you'll find that no one had more fun playing the game.

Blasé Easterners were shocked right down to their high-button shoes in the 1928 Cup final at Hamilton between the Tigers and Regina Roughriders who were making the first of five consecutive Cup challenges. Two Roughies ran onto the field with their bare legs showing. In some sophisticated circles, chroniclers of the day reported, "consternation was rife." Never before had the East seen legs bared on a football field.

Sports writers referred to the two Roughrider players as "daredevils" and one noted in his report that "they escaped without injury." If nothing else, this leg nudity started a trend and 27 years later — in 1955 — an edict was issued to all Cup-competing teams: "Bare legs aren't a pretty sight on a football field," CRU President Ken Montgomery of Edmonton solemnly declared. "Players in future Cup games must wear stockings. Who wants to look at men in their bare legs?"

This 1928 game was another shocker for the West. The Roughriders had been beaten 54-0 in 1923 by Queen's University on their last trip East and this time they were knocked over 30-0. To strengthen for this one they recruited five players from Regina's junior Pats — Eddie (Dynamite) James, Andy (Red) Currie, Jim Doctor, quarterback Angie Mitchell and punter Sol Bloomfield. Even without these men the Roughies had been a power in the West, unbeaten and without a touchdown scored against them in three years.

But these were the famed Tigers, one of the toughest and roughest seen. One player was Brian Timmis who had always refused to wear a helmet. A great plunger, he drove over for two touchdowns in this game. So did Jimmy Simpson, Hamilton's young end playing his first season of organized football.

And back again as coach was Mike Rodden. He considered this club the greatest he had ever seen and Eastern sports writers agreed. But they were also, for a change, impressed with the Roughriders even though they had been soundly beaten.

Only 4,767 spectators watched the game at Hamilton and they witnessed some sort of Cup history. Pep Leadlay drop-kicked three converts.

Then came the depression in 1929, and, for the first time, forward passes were thrown in a Cup final. The pass was legal in the West only. The East still had to discover that it was a quick-striking, exciting and crowd-pleasing play to watch. One of the rules of this dynamic new offence was that a pass could not be thrown within 25 yards of the opposition's goal line. The restriction finally was removed in 1936 when the Canadian Rugby Union decided it was time the East got in line with the West and ruled it could be thrown from anywhere on the field.

Regina Roughriders, again Western champions, met the Tigers at Hamilton on Nov. 30, 1929, under the worst possible weather conditions and lost 14-3. Driving snow and freezing temperatures had turned the field into a block of ice and there were only 100 fans in their seats when the game started. Other spectators swarmed around under the stands and dashed up to seats for brief moments to watch the action. The paid attendance was 1,906 and hundreds who couldn't take the bitter cold left the stadium before half time.

Roughriders, again coached by Al Ritchie, tried 11 passes and gained about 100 yards. Tigers tried one late in the game, Huck Welch to Jimmy Simpson, for a touchdown but it was not allowed. From that day on Mike Rodden claimed that his team, specifically Welch and Simpson, had been robbed of a spot in Cup history. "I've never charged that umpire Priestley of Winnipeg was dishonest," Rodden said years later. "But he called that touchdown back because he said it had been completed within the 25-yard line. Because of the snow, I don't know how he could even see the play."

Mike, of course, was indulging in a bit of needling. It was a good bet he couldn't see the play himself from the sidelines. Ritchie, too, had a couple of beefs. He had taken great pains to ensure that his Roughriders would be playing within the Eastern rules at all times. He wrote to Shag Shaughnessy of McGill University in Montreal and Billy Hughes of Queen's University for their playbooks. There were a couple of plays the Roughriders had not used and that Ritchie had decided to try against Hamilton. "We hadn't heard about it out in the West, but a couple of weeks before we arrived in Hamilton the Eastern officials had thrown out both plays," said Ritchie. "They were illegal before we ever tried them."

It was the first time that rules interpretations had cropped up in Cup play — but certainly not the last. The big committee-room East-West fights were still to come. But now, in 1929, Roughriders and Ritchie were disappointed in more than the score, the weather and rules interpretations. Total game receipts, including 42 tickets sold to a group of transplanted Westerners living in Hamilton, were only $2,537.42. After game expenses, Regina received $1,400 and it cost them nearly $2,000 to make the trip. The Twenties had ended on a sad note indeed for the West.

CHAPTER IV

THE BITTER EAST - WEST FIGHT

The Early Thirties

It seemed that the Canadian Rugby Union went out of its way to antagonize the West in this depression-hit period. It refused for seven years to adopt forward pass rules suggested by the West and then, in 1933, cut the Winnipegs out of an automatic berth in the Grey Cup final. Not strong enough, said the CRU, after looking over the 0-9 won-lost record of the West in national play since 1921.

Instead, it ruled that the Western champions would have to play a sudden-death semi-final in the East, an unprecedented procedure. Apart from this unpleasant business, and the fact that total Cup attendance in the 1930-34 period barely got past the 25,000-mark, milestones were established every year. The West scored its first touchdown in East-West play in 1930. The first Cup touchdown pass was thrown in 1931. In 1932, Regina Roughriders lost for the fifth consecutive year, a record, and in 1934 game officials tooted notes on their horns to denote a rule infraction. Previously, whistles were used.

Freddie Brown of the Regina Roughriders accomplished in one brief, exhilarating moment what no other player from the West had been able to do in six previous East-West games. He scored the West's first touchdown in the Cup final against Toronto Balmy Beach at Toronto. It came in the third quarter with Beaches ahead 10-6 and, carrying statistics a little farther, his five points equalled the total scoring of the West in all those discouraging years. The total count up to Freddie's gallop over an Eastern goal line was: East 158 points, West 5.

Regina lost 11-6 and, unfortunately, details of Brown's historic play are somewhat obscure because newspapers of the day didn't bother to detail such happenings. "Everyone looked at the Monday

39

papers casually as though it had just been a post-season exhibition game," wrote Ted Reeve, Toronto Telegram sports columnist, years later. Reeve, with the Beaches in 1930, shared personal honors with Brown. The Moaner shrugged off a shoulder separation to make the big play that saved the day for the East. It came in the final minutes on a play that fans talked about for years.

The Roughriders appeared to be on the way to a touchdown that, with the convert, would put them ahead 12-11 and, who knows, win the Cup. And Beaches were hurt. Ab Box, who later went to Toronto Argonauts, was lost through a leg injury in the opening quarter. The Beaches' ace punter, who had kicked three singles before his injury, watched the game from the bench. With him was Reeve. The big fellow had suffered his shoulder injury the previous week in the Eastern final against Hamilton and was riding the bench this day until Regina moved deep into Beach territory. The Toronto defence held and Roughriders were forced to punt. Before left-footed Sol Bloomfield could loft the ball over a flock of onrushing Beaches, it slammed crazily off a hurtling player. Reeve.

The pressure was off. That was the ball game. Of course, it was a typical Balmy Beach day — cold and overcast and the field was muddy. The crowd at Varsity Stadium was only 3,914 and gate receipts totalled a mere $4,066.50. The CRU, fully aware of the drawing power of the pesky Beaches and the Roughriders, decided to do something about it in 1930. It scheduled a doubleheader for the only time in Cup history. As a curtain-raiser, the CRU staged the national junior championship and Toronto Argonauts defeated Winnipeg Native Sons 7-1.

By 1931, it was getting so the West, particularly Regina, would do almost anything in an effort to win the Cup. Roughriders had borrowed Eastern club playbooks in 1929 and were forced to abandon a couple of plays when the CRU declared they were illegal. In 1931 they had won the Western title with a ground attack that was thought to be formidable enough to win the big one against the Winged Wheelers at Montreal on Dec. 5. Team officials held lengthy skull sessions to devise game plans. Finally, someone had a bright idea.

The attack would be even more fearsome if sharp leather cleats were attached to the players' boots. With added traction, the Roughies just might topple the favored Winged Wheelers. But it was late — the night before the game. While Montreal slept on the eve of this

40

city's first Cup final, the shoemaker worked. He had been paid $67 for the job, by no means a minor expenditure in these days of low-budget clubs. But Roughriders figured the outlay would be well worth it if only they could take the trophy for a train ride and let Western fans see what they had been fighting for all these years.

After making the deal with the cobbler, club officials went to bed secure in the knowledge that at last they had found a secret weapon that just might whip the East. A few hours before the kickoff, Rough-riders packed their new shoes and headed confidently for the stadium. It wouldn't be legal, but it would have been much better if they had carried their skates. The field was frozen hard with patches of glaring ice. Wheelers trotted out for the pre-game warmup in sneakers while the Roughriders, morose and downhearted, looked down at their spiked boots. The cleats had no traction. The Wheelers' basketball shoes were ideally suited for the type of going.

And Wheelers had their own secret weapon — a young man from Syracuse, imported this season. Warren Stevens had infuriated Eastern opponents with the pass all year. The historic first Cup touchdown pass went 40 yards from Stevens to Kenny Grant in the third quarter. Stevens further confounded the Westerners on the convert try. He held the ball for Huck Welch, Montreal's great punter who had left Hamilton Tigers this year. Gordie Perry broke for the goal line and Stevens took the snap, jumped up, faded back for a pass and then took a clear road over the goal line to score the extra point. Although the forward pass was one of Montreal's better weapons, the Wheelers put emphasis on the kicking of Welch. He kicked two singles, a convert and a field goal in the 22-0 victory.

Regina's line attack was effective and the club more than held its own along the ground despite those shoes. The only jarring note for the East happened at the final whistle. The Wheelers' Red Tellier swiped a page from Regina's book and belted George Gilhooley of the Roughriders. Red was banished from football for life but three years later the CRU relented and he was reinstated. It was the only Cup final to result in suspension of a player.

Roughriders, of course, were astonished at Tellier's behavior. Their linemen had been planting fists in their opposite number's faces on the final play of games for years. They had discarded the practice in the Cup final and here was one of their own players having to smile at the world with store teeth showing.

Roughriders were back again in 1932, this time against the Tigers at Hamilton, for a game that proved only one point: Roughriders showed a remarkable capacity for absorbing Cup beatings. They lost 25-6 for their fifth consecutive East-West loss and Ritchie's fourth straight setback as coach. Ritchie felt that Roughriders could go all the way with virtually an all-Canadian lineup and, although he had a couple of imports, he didn't go along with the idea adopted by Winnipeg this year that Americans were necessary if the West expected to defeat the East. Take quarterback Angie Mitchell. He grew up in Regina, learned his football there and led Roughriders to six Cup finals.

"Angie could always play 60 minutes with no trouble," Ritchie said years later. "He was just a little fellow, but he could throw nice short passes." But Regina's determination, Ritchie's dreams and Angie's nice short passes weren't enough to contain the Tigers. Brian Timmis was nearing the end of a brilliant career as a plunger in this game, tearing holes in the Regina line as he rushed for 105 yards. Teammate Dave Sprague bulled for 95 yards.

Tigers tossed only two passes for 48 yards. They concentrated on their specialty, muscular ball-carrying, and gained 376 yards from scrimmage. So awesome were the Riders that Ritchie felt their reputation did as much harm as their ball-carrying. His Roughies, he said, suffered from stage fright. They also scored the second touchdown for the West in the Cup — a fourth-quarter score by Phat DeFrate, converted by Curt Schave. Three opposing players in this game were to go into officiating after their playing careers ended. Hamilton's Seymour Wilson became possibly the best-known referee in the East. Another was Jimmy Simpson of the Tigers who eventually became trainer of Hamilton clubs after a stint at officiating.

Regina's Cliff Roseborough became a veteran referee in the West. He was to take part in 17 Cup finals, seven as a player and 10 as an official, before retiring in 1964.

Roughriders gave way to import-conscious Winnipegs in 1933. Then came the incredible CRU decision that robbed Winnipegs of their rightful place in the East-West final. It came about when the CRU backed off from a decisive showdown with the all-powerful Eastern Big Four Union. Big Four teams, in effect, told the CRU to get lost while they conducted their own business, an unprecedented two-game total-point series for the league championship instead of the established sudden-death format.

The Western champions, the Ontario Rugby Football Union, Eastern college union champions — and the Cup final itself — would have to wait. And the CRU said okay. The Union muffed a chance to assert its authority as the governing body of football in Canada by demanding that the Big Four get things over with in a hurry or forget about a possible Cup berth. Instead, it compromised and Winnipegs suffered.

Here are the circumstances: Toronto Argonauts and Montreal Winged Wheelers had ended the Big Four schedule in a first-place deadlock and decided to play the two-game total-point series before advancing into the Eastern semi-final against either the ORFU Sarnia Imperials or the college champion University of Toronto Blues. Their reasoning was a simple matter of economics. They had a good thing going for them with sell-out crowds assured for the two games and they were much more interested in the revenue from these than in a hit-and-miss proposition at the gate against either the Imperials or Blues. It was late in the season and Varsity bowed out of the picture.

The collegians said they could not extend their football schedule into December and packed their gear. This, along with the no-compromise attitude of the Big Four clubs, made things that much easier for the CRU. It ruled that Sarnia would receive the bye into the Cup final and Winnipegs would meet the Toronto-Montreal winner in the Eastern semi-final.

Confusing? Indeed it was, considering that the only logical move was to schedule a meeting between the Big Four champion and Sarnia with the winner advancing against Winnipegs for Earl Grey's trophy. Argonauts beat Montreal 5-4 and 15-5. The Argos, coached by Lew Hayman from Syracuse in his rookie year in Canadian football, were a crowd-pleasing, dipsy-doodling club known as probably the greatest opportunists in the game.

They had a fine knack of placing players at the right spots at the right times. Besides, the club was warming up as the weather became colder. And there was a suspicion that Hayman and the Argo Bounce had arrived simultaneously on the Toronto football scene. That was only half right. The Argo Bounce was to come later.

Against this background, and certainly not happy with the CRU and the switch from the traditional Grey Cup format of sending the

43

Western champions directly into the Canadian final, Winnipegs travelled East.

They had tapped the mid-Western United States for players in 1932 and again this year and there was no doubt they were the powerhouse in the West. Notre Dame grad Carl Cronin was playing coach. Russ Rebholz of Wisconsin tossed the passes and looked after the punting and Greg (Hardrock) Kabat, another Wisconsin grad, bossed the line. These three, backed up with some solid performers, shattered the defending champion Regina Roughriders in the Western semi-final 11-1. They moved into the final against Calgary Altomahs, won 15-1, and fussed and fidgeted for weeks while the CRU and the Big Four conducted their wordy war.

Finally, on Dec. 2 at Varsity Stadium in Toronto and with 8,359 fans in attendance, they were keyed up to take Argos and head for Sarnia for a Dec. 9 meeting with the mighty Imperials.

The pass was Winnipeg's big weapon and time and again the Westerners drove deep into Argonaut territory only to be blunted by some spectacular play by the Boatmen. They also had the extension play and twice Teddy Morris, who had played for Winnipeg Native Sons juniors in 1930, popped in to intercept laterals and gallop 80 and 90 yards that pulled Argos out of deep trouble.

Winnipegs lost 13-0, but the score certainly didn't tell the story. Argos — and the East — had a real scare and the CRU, somewhat abashed at the decision it had made, changed its mind in a hurry. It reinstated the Western champions as automatic Cup finalists in 1934. Winnipegs headed for home and Argonauts high-tailed it to Sarnia for a memorable battle with the Imps who had such stars as Norm Perry, Alex Hayes, Hugh (Bummer) Stirling, Claude Harris, Pat Butler, Rocky Parsaca, Gord Patterson, Johnny Manore and a host of others.

It was a frigid, 14-above afternoon, the field was coated with snow and the ground was frozen. Agros were lucky to get out of this one alive and only inches separated Imperials from possible victory and a certain tie in the final minute of play. Here's how one Toronto writer described Argonauts' 4-3 victory: "Argonauts were soundly whipped along the wingline, decisively overpowered at the ends and outshone in the backfield."

How did they manage to win? They came up with the big plays when they were needed. In the third quarter, for instance, Tuffy Griffiths barrelled through the middle of the line to block a Sarnia punt. This set up a field goal by Tommy Burns, the giant all-Eastern middle, later known as a tackle.

The inches gambit occurred when Perry gathered in a pass from Parsaca, veered toward the sidelines and tight-roped down to the Toronto five-yard line. Ab Box, who just a minute earlier had booted a towering single to break the 3-3 deadlock, caught him. There was time for one more play and Imps were getting ready to line up for a field goal attempt. But, hold on.

Jo-Jo Stirrett, a University of Toronto player in the early 1920s and now a Sarnia resident and game official, ruled that Perry's foot had slipped out of touch back on the Toronto 42. The call put the Imps out of reach to punt for the game-tying single. Stirling, certainly one of the finest punters seen on a football field, had kicked singles in the second, third and fourth quarters.

Argonauts had had to win two tough ones, but nothing could be taken away from them. Hot-potato football was Hayman's style and he had the players to make it work, speedy young backs who flipped the ball around on the three-man extension play that chilled and thrilled fans. They had provided a wide-open brand of football and oldtimers wagged their heads in disbelief. They had warned all along that the lateral was too risky and that Lew would find himself — and Argos — in all sorts of trouble on interceptions and fumbles. But Lew was willing to take those chances and they paid off.

No one could blame him with the gang he had. Here are a few: Box, Burns, Joe Wright, Jimmy Keith, Morris, Wes Cutler, Jim Palmer, Jack Taylor, Frank Tindall, Andy Mullan, Art Upper, Sparky Vail, Armour Munro, Lou Snyder, Len Staughton, Bill Wilson, Griffiths, Mike Chepesuik, Dave Ferris.

A couple of bands were in attendance in the 1934 final at Toronto, but the most prominent musicians were umpire Hec Crighton and head linesman Hal DeGruchy. They couldn't play a tune, but they could make a lot of noise on their horns. It was a new twist in officiating designed to cut down on the number of whistles and stoppages of play. A blow on the horn, which was to be replaced by a fluttering handkerchief in 1949, meant play continued but that an infraction had been committed.

Previously, umpires and head linesmen were empowered to stop play. This meant the games sputtered along with stops and starts every time there was an infraction. Now, only the referee was equipped with a whistle. And the ref this time was Angie Mitchell, former quarterback with the Roughriders. Here he was in a neutral role as Regina squared off against Sarnia. The Westerners, as seen by some knowledgeable football men, were described as the best team yet to come out of the Prairies. But the ORFU Imperials were still the same cool, methodical and almost nonchalant force that had been a power in Canadian football for years.

Bummer Stirling was back. So was Orm Beach, the Kansas giant; elusive, fleet-footed Mike Hedgewick, experienced Alex Hayes, Norm Perry, and many others. They had won their fourth straight ORFU title this year, and the end was nowhere in sight. Imperials eventually ran the string to nine straight, ending in 1940 when Toronto Balmy Beach took over.

That would be the end of the Imps' glory days, except for league title runs in 1951 and 1952 when the ORFU, reduced to farm-club status by the Big Four and Western Conference teams, were soundly whipped. Fan support dwindled alarmingly and the ORFU quietly folded. The only tears shed were those by men who had played in the league in its finest hours and by the men who had carefully nursed it along.

But the Imperials' nine-straight titles — 1931-39 — established a mark that probably never will be matched by any team in any league in the country. This year — 1934 — Imperials, still stung over their 4-3 heart-breaking loss to Argonauts in 1933, weren't taking any chances. Some day someone would point to a football on a mantle and offer it as evidence of why the Regina Roughriders were thwarted 20-12. Stirling beat the Westerners with his kicking.

The ball on the mantle would be the one he punted high into the crowd on his first kick of the afternoon. One of the 8,900 fans walked out of Varsity Stadium with the ball snuggled under his coat. Stirling kicked five singles as the Western boys watched in awe. But Regina had some stars of its own, the most prominent being Ralph Pierce whom Ritchie called one of the greatest imports to play in Canada.

And fans saw the last display of drop kicking, an art that had been dormant and was about to die. Alex Hayes drop-kicked two converts and a field goal for Sarnia. Not since the great Pep Leadlay of Queen's University and Hamilton Tiger fame had there been such a kicking show in a Cup game.

It was the last game, too, for Perry. The Sarnia galloper, known as "The Golden Ghost of The Gridiron," ended his brilliant 15-year career. He was to become president of the CRU in 1953 and a few years later football mourned his death. Regina's 12 points were the most scored by a Western club since these East-West finals started in 1921 and it was the first time the West had scored two touchdowns in the big game.

Regina's strong showing should have been a serious warning to the East. The East had a 10-0 won-lost Cup record against Western clubs and blasé Easterners could see no reason why this sort of thing couldn't go on indefinitely.

They were wrong.

CHAPTER V

THE HOT DOG CHAMPIONS

Dec. 7, 1935, at Hamilton
Winnipeg 18, Hamilton Tigers 12

Grey Cup days were always the same. And there was no reason to change the routine as far as this East-West final was concerned — the 11th since 1921.

Players on Eastern championship teams dined with their families at home and hustled over to the stadium for another game. They had beaten the West every time out, celebrated over sandwiches and beer, packed their gear for another season and continued their normal way of life.

There were no great post-game celebrations, city hall receptions, hail-to-the-champions parades. The East had done what comes naturally: Accommodate the Western challenges after cleaning up in the East. There was nothing to suggest that Western football fans should circle this cold, bleak, overcast, rainy Dec. 7 on their calendars as another historic day to rank with such significant achievements as invention of the safety pin, the automobile, the discovery of insulin or the first trans-Atlantic flight.

That is, until about 4 p.m. at the old Hamilton Amateur Athletic Association grounds when a group of players who had lived on a diet of hot dogs for days scrambled to their dressing room as Canadian champions. Make that Grey Cup champions. The West had won its first Grey Cup. Winnipegs rattled and shook the dice and won everything on their first roll. It didn't make any difference that the pot was short, that there wasn't enough to pay their bills and get out of town.

The West at last had beaten the smug East. The West was fully aware of the East's casual attitude toward the national final games. So it probably wasn't much of a surprise to treasurer G. Sydney Halter of the Winnipegs on Friday night when he was passing the time in a

Hamilton sports store to see a burly policeman walk in for a chat. The cop was Bill Friday, a Tiger lineman who had a beat to cover until 8 a.m. He would grab a couple of hours sleep after work and then report to the stadium.

Winnipegs, undefeated in the West all season, had been east a week. They had settled in at Detroit, played a mid-week exhibition game in Windsor against Assumption College and showed absolutely nothing although they had won 17-0. They were so bad that Eastern sports writers on the scene thought that the players should have been at least introduced to each other before they left home. Some were in the wrong places at the wrong times and the bookmakers, as usual, installed the Tigers 5-to-1 favorites to win the Cup.

The Easterners didn't know that some of those three-footed Winnipeggers were not playing their regular positions against Assumption. The odds undoubtedly would have lengthened if they had known that the Westerners were living on a diet of hot dogs. Years later, Halter recalled that the players had been given a choice — "either they could eat in the hotel or we would give them a dollar a meal and let them eat wherever they wanted. They took the dollar. They'd eat a couple of hot dogs and have enough left over for a show."

Eastern football fans followed the usual script of waiting until game day to decide whether they would pay up to $1.60 to watch their heroes win another game or pass it up and read about it in the Monday newspapers. The weather was a big factor in their decision and a rainy, overcast Grey Cup morning settled the issue. They would stay at home. As a result only 6,405 persons turned up for a contest that brought the East crashing to earth. It was a day that Fritz Hanson, a 150-pound blond flash from North Dakota State College, became a legend in Canadian football and the Winnipegs, which cost an impressive $7,500 to put together, helped to make the Grey Cup the biggest event in the nation's sporting life.

Winnipegs, with seven American imports in the lineup, not only won the game but whipped the mighty Tigers in every department. The 22-year-old Hanson, alternately slipping, sliding and speeding in the goo, ran punts back more than 300 yards. And, with Winnipegs ahead 12-10 in the third quarter, he streaked 78 yards for the touchdown that locked up the game for the West. Time after time Hanson left Tigers' outside wings Jimmy Simpson and Seymour Wilson clawing in the mud. When long, high Frank Turville punts zoomed over the AAA stadium and started falling toward Hanson, the Hamilton pair raced in on him.

Each time Fritzie did a little jig in the goo, watched the ends sail past him, then started up the field. Seven times he returned kicks 35 to 50 yards. Tigers gained only 48 yards rushing against 125 for the Westerners and Tigers completed only two passes for 38 yards against three for 87 for Winnipeg. While Hanson was a one-man powerhouse, others contributed to Winnipegs' victory. Here is the lineup:

Bob Fritz from Concordia College in Moorhead, Minn., was the quarterback. Hanson, Greg Kabat and Russ Rebholz from Wisconsin and Eddie (Dynamite) James, a former Regina Roughrider, comprised the backs. Lou (Rosy) Adelman was the centre. The guards were Dr. Bert Oja from Minnesota and Eddie Kushner. At tackle were Herb Peschel from North Dakota State, and Lou Mogul. Ends were Bud Marquardt from North Dakota and Joe Perpich. Reserves were Cliff Roseborough, Jeff Nicklin, Arni Coulter, Slush Harris, Dr. Tubber Kobrinsky, Bill Ceretti, Dave Harding, Dick Lane, Eric Law, Herb Mobberley, Nick Pagones, Johnny Patrick.

The victory was particularly sweet for Rosy Adelman. He was the only holdover from the 1925 Winnipeg Tammany Tigers who had lost 24-1 to Ottawa Senators and he vividly recalled the panning the Tigers had received from Eastern reporters who had called the Westerners a bunch of "intermediates." Although the Hamilton Tigers were prohibitive favorites to trample the Winnipegs, there was one dissenting voice. Rocky Parsaca, a standout with Sarnia Imperials, had gone West earlier in the year with the ORFU champions and had been beaten 3-1 by the Winnipegs.

"It could go all the way," he said on his return East and in the days before the Cup final. "This Winnipeg team is pretty good." But hardly anyone listened, even when it was pointed out that Winnipegs' victory over the 1934 Cup champions marked the first time a Western senior club had defeated an Eastern team. And Imperials were by no means pushovers. They had won the ORFU title and had lost 22-3 to Tigers in the Eastern final.

Tigers, coached by Fred Veale, had loads of talent, including: Brian Timmis, Johnny Ferraro, Huck Welch, Frank Turville, Bernie Thornton, Eddie Wright, Don Summerhayes, Bill Friday, Pony Stull, Wilf Patterson, John Craig, George Mountain, Jimmy (Red) Dunn, Rus Blum, John Agnew, Jerry Brock, Jim Smiley, Norm Mountain, Boily

Jeffries, Bus Reed and, of course, Seymour Wilson and Jimmy Simpson.

Here is the scoring summary:

First quarter
1. Winnipegs, touchdown (Bud Marquardt)
2. Hamilton, field goal (Frank Turville)

Second Quarter
3. Winnipegs, touchdown (Greg Kabat)
4. Winnipegs, convert (Russ Rebholz)
5. Hamilton, single (Frank Turville)
6. Winnipegs, single (Greg Kabat)

Third Quarter
7. Hamilton, touchdown (Wilf Patterson)
8. Hamilton, single (Frank Turville)
9. Winnipegs, touchdown (Fritz Hanson)
10. Winnipegs, convert (Russ Rebholz)

Fourth Quarter
11. Hamilton, safety touch

When it was all over, Winnipegs found they didn't have enough money to pay their hotel bill and the transportation home. Gate receipts were only $5,583.92 plus $100 for broadcasting rights. "To get out of town," Halter said years later, "we had to ask a football fan named Les Isard to pay our hotel bill. Everybody was happy because we had won but I was trying to figure out how we'd make up the $2,000 it cost us to make the trip."

Many stories were to be repeated over and over about Winnipegs. One of the most popular, and the one that grew taller as the years went by, concerned the club's trip home. When the players discovered that Fritz Kreisler was on the same train, they badgered the sleeping-car conductor into giving them his compartment number. It was only fitting, they reasoned, that the two big-league Fritz's should meet.

They hammered on the world-famed violinist's door and, so the story goes, he poked his head out and said: "Sorry, but I'm too tired to play." "Well, then," said the football-playing Fritz, "yeh don't have to play a real number. Just twang up the fiddle and practise a little." "I don't practice," replied Kreisler.

"Yeh don't practice," exclaimed Hanson.

"Mr. Kreisler, how the hell do you expect to amount to anything?" And the story people tell of 1936 in Canadian football is not a tall tale. And, certainly, not a bit funny.

CHAPTER VI

THE ANGRY WEST

Dec. 5, 1936, at Toronto
Sarnia Imperials 26, Ottawa Rough Riders 20

The Grey Cup went for another long ride, this time from West to East without a Western football player in sight. But the jeering from the West was enough to turn the air blue all the way from Regina to Toronto.

The only thing that bothered the otherwise inscrutable Canadian Rugby Union officials was the all-powerful Amateur Athletic Union which, in these days, had iron-fisted control over most amateur sport in the country, even football. The AAU eventually was to disintegrate but here, in the mid-30s, their directors together with the CRU and Eastern clubs had noted the influx of Americans to Western teams and decided that something had to be done fast before the Yankees took over. The CRU with a nudge from Eastern clubs, decided to put a stop to this importation of Americans.

Only American residents of Canada before Jan. 1 were eligible to play, it ruled. The Big Four had banned 10 imports just four days before the start of its schedule to meet the edict. The West, dependent on imports as it had been in 1935 when Winnipegs, with seven Americans on its roster, had beaten Hamilton Tigers 18-12 in the Cup final, didn't go along with the fuzzy ruling.

The CRU also ruled that teams could have a maximum of only five imports. Regina Roughriders, who had knocked off Winnipegs in the Western playoffs, prepared to travel east but the people who governed the game said no, you didn't abide by the regulations. Roughriders had five ineligible players on the team and officials volunteered to drop them and to make the trip. Too late, said the CRU. The screaming started, but the CRU was adamant and finally Regina coach Al Ritchie, the man who had taken Roughrider teams east year after year in the late 1920s and early 1930s, gave up. "Let them declare their cheese champions," he said.

Events in the East had reached the comical stage in 1935 involving Ottawa. Jimmy McCaffrey, a twinkly-eyed Irishman who later was known affectionately as the East's Con Man, had been suspended — along with his entire Rough Rider executive — by the AAU over an import. James P. got into trouble over a player named Roy Berry who was really Bohn Hilliard. Confusing? Indeed it was, especially to hear McCaffrey's explanation years later.

Hilliard, an American signed by Ottawa, was to receive $900 a season — under the table, of course. But Hilliard told McCaffrey he had once played International League baseball. That made him a pro.

"I told him that if he knew of anyone else to have him get in touch with me," explained McCaffrey. It wasn't long before a "friend" of Hilliard's, a Roy Berry, offered his services. Berry played the entire season for Ottawa. What happened was that Hilliard really did have a friend named Berry and he went to the trouble of exchanging identities. McCaffrey denied he knew anything of the deception.

On another occasion he talked his way out of trouble when it was discovered that another import had played pro football. He said the player had been under the impression that Canadian rules were similar to those used in English cricket. He was called onto the carpet by the Big Four executive. But James P. had done his homework. "In England," he solemnly told dumbfounded officials, "it's perfectly all right to play together. If you're a pro, you come out of the gate marked 'Players.' If you're an amateur, you use the gate marked 'Gentlemen.' "

He was right. And Jimmy, who was to enliven the scene for many years before his death, wasn't suspended. When Ottawa went into the 1936 Cup game, McCaffrey and his executive were at the helm, thanks to a visit he had made to the home of the AAU president before the season opened. After several hours of explanation, helped by liquid refreshment that McCaffrey happened to have along, all was forgiven.

"The last thing I remember was the train moving out of the station and the president of the AAU running along the platform," McCaffrey recalled. "He was shouting 'Don't worry, McCaffrey, don't worry. You're a good fellow. Everything will be all right.' " The Cup game was a dandy, one of the most exciting in Cup history. The Imperials,

ORFU champions for the sixth consecutive year, jumped into a 12-5 lead in the opening quarter, Riders tied it 12-12 in the second and the Imps moved ahead 26-12 in the third and held on to win.

Favored Ottawa, even with Jim McCaffrey and his executive back in harness, couldn't do much right in this one. It was Imperials' last fling at the Cup and they bowed out with a fine record — two Cup victories in three appearances. This year, too, marked the exit of collegiate clubs in the hunt for the trophy. The University of Toronto won the college group and defaulted to Ottawa. In 1937, the Intercollegiate Union made it official — no more challenges. In 1937, too, Winnipeg was back. The club had changed its name to the Blue Bombers. They were a powerhouse but the East had a secret weapon. People called it the Argonaut Bounce.

CHAPTER VII

THE ARGO BOUNCE

Dec. 11, 1937, at Toronto
Toronto Argonauts 4, Winnipeg Blue Bombers 3

When this game ended, Argonauts should have packed their gear and headed directly for the gaming tables. The Bombers would have been delighted to stake them.

With Argos' luck they couldn't help but roll straight sevens. If it wasn't luck that gave Argos the Cup you could at least say the club was extremely fortunate. Even the staunchest Double Blue fans would admit this, perhaps grudgingly, because the Scullers, coached by Lew Hayman, were a powerhouse that only a week earlier had fought a stirring battle to beat the defending Cup champion Sarnia Imperials 10-6 in the sudden-death Eastern final.

The Toronto club had discovered a new touch, one that was to be described down the years as the Argonaut Bounce. They received all sorts of help to salvage this one but, as any sports expert will tell you: Take a look at the scoreboard. Blue Bombers and their fans did on this 23-degree afternoon at Varsity Stadium, and they could hardly believe the story it had to tell. Toronto 4 Winnipeg 3. Game over. The umpire was Eddie Grant. He had scored Winnipeg Tammany Tigers' lone point in the 1925 Cup final when the Tigers, as the Winnipeg club then was known, lost 24-1 to Ottawa Senators.

Undoubtedly, during the long winter months ahead, Eddie must have booted himself for taking the game assignment. This was the situation: In the opening quarter, Argonauts' Bill Stukus fumbled on the Toronto seven-yard line and a flock of Bombers and Argonauts dove for the ball. Grant was right on top of the play. Referee Hec Crighton of Toronto, following downfield, ran up to Grant and asked: "Whose ball?" Grant was so upset he couldn't speak. Crighton repeated the question and the Winnipeg official blurted: "I—I don't know."

Faced with the need of instant decision, and 11,522 spectators on

55

their feet and yelling, Crighton made a decision: Argos' ball, he said, reasoning that they would have been hurt most by losing possession near their goal line. "There was nothing else for me to do," he recalled years later. If this wasn't enough to ensure that Grant would become a most unpopular fellow at home, he clinched it later in the same quarter. He called back a Winnipeg touchdown, and again on a play involving Bill Stukus.

Stuke got under a Winnipeg punt at the Argonaut 20-yard line and dropped the ball when tackled hard by Bud Marquardt. Bill Ceretti of the Bombers scooped up the loose ball and ran over Argos' line for the touchdown. But just a minute. Grant had tooted his horn to denote an infraction on the play. His ruling: Stukus hadn't been given the necessary five yards on the kick.

Still in the first quarter Fritzie Hanson, whose fantastic running two years previously had given the West its first Grey Cup, fumbled at the Winnipeg 20-yard line after taking a punt. Three Argonaut players were right there, the ball took just the right bounce and popped into Bill Byers' arms. On the next play, Earl Selkirk kicked a 31-yard field goal.

Later in the game, Marquardt blocked a Toronto punt and Teddy Morris galloped after the loose ball with Marquardt right behind him. Teddy moved in front as the ball took a hop. Let Teddy tell it: "The ball bounced right up into my hands. That was the Argo bounce. Anyway, it saved the day for us. Winnipeg would have had first down on our 25 if Marquardt had recovered it and, the way those Bombers were going, it could have ended in a Winnipeg touchdown."

The Bombers certainly were the powerhouse of the West and they arrived in Toronto without imports Ole Midgarten and Martin Gainor. Neither was eligible because of the Jan. 1 residence rule. They did, however, still have seven imports in the lineup and most of the players had been on the history-making 1935 squad. Quarterback Bob Fritz, also the coach, was one of Winnipeg's best. His field generalship kept Bombers on the march, but they had to contend with a 22-year-old punter named Bob Isbister of Argos. He averaged 52.3 yards a kick, a Cup record that still stands.

Still in that first quarter Isbister stopped what appeared to be a sure Winnipeg touchdown. Fritz had picked up an Argo fumble and had raced 65 yards before Isbister hauled him down on the Toronto 10-yard line. The Bombers had to settle for a single by Steve Olander who added another point in the second quarter. Greg Kabat scored Winnipeg's final point in the third period. Argo bounce or no Argo bounce, Toronto had to win a tough one to get the Grey Cup.

CHAPTER VIII

THE RED STOREY SAGA

Dec. 10, 1938, at Toronto
Toronto Argonauts 30, Winnipeg Blue Bombers 7

Argonauts didn't need their famous bounce in this game. They had Roy Alvin (Red) Storey. To some motorists in the crowd of 18,778 at Varsity Stadium, the big red-headed kid warming up with Argos might have looked vaguely familiar.

He was the same gangling youngster who, for three years, had thumbed rides from his home in Barrie to Toronto for Argonaut practices. Motorists along the 50-mile stretch of highway couldn't mistake him. He always wore his Argo sweater. And certainly Reg Threlfall, the nonstop-talking coach of the Bombers, had never seen or heard of this 19-year-old. Threlfall arrived in Toronto a few days before the game and summarily dismissed Argonauts with the observation that "we'll cut 'em off at the knees and they'll look like Boy Scouts."

The first to agree was Argo Coach Lew Hayman, a sad-faced individual. "He may be right," said Lew. "My boys are in terrible shape. But we'll make an appearance and I hope they'll do okay." When the teams left the field, the Argo knees were intact. And the players were in good shape, except possibly Roy Alvin Storey who was a little winded.

He had collected little more than bench slivers during his three years with the club. In 15 electrifying minutes — in the final quarter to be exact — he almost single-handedly demolished the Bombers. Red scored three touchdowns, set the stage for another and turned the game into a one-man blitz. Bombers led 7-5 going into that fateful period — until Hayman told Red to get in there. Before the afternoon was over, people would laugh if you told them that (a) Red had a sister who was once a better football player than he was and (b) just a few years earlier his high school football coach in Barrie told him to "get out of here before you get killed."

This happened when Red was a 95-pound stripling. He heeded his coach's advice and went back to his neighborhood club — the Tiffin Street Terrors — where his tom-boyish sister, Irene, was the star halfback and punter. Red filled out fast. He sprouted to a brawny six-foot-three 200-pounder and Teddy Morris, then with Argonauts, flushed him out of Barrie and brought him to Toronto. He was a big green kid playing among men — and only as a lowly substitute.

That was his role until the fourth quarter of this Winnipeg-Argonaut game when Hayman, desperate for fresh bodies, peered down the bench and spotted Red. The kid was on his feet and roaring out onto the field before Hayman could blink. Quarterback Bill Stukus decided to gamble on a play Argos hadn't used all season, and with unknown Storey as the ball carrier. Red hit the line and didn't stop until he had crossed the Winnipeg goal line 28 yards away, dragging safety Fritzie Hanson with him the last few yards.

The stubborn, dead-tired Bombers took to the air and Bud Marquardt appeared to be under a pass when Storey soared to make an interception. The young dynamo didn't stop running for 40 yards — Touchdown No. 2. Red was just warming up. He later took a lateral from Bob Isbister and romped 102 yards, paving the way for a touchdown by Bernie Thornton. And when the redhead recovered his wind, he ran 12 yards for his third touchdown.

Years later, when asked why Argos' hadn't let him take a crack at the touchdown after his long run, Red replied simply: "I was too pooped." This game started Red on a brilliant career. New York Giants offered him a contract but he turned it down because, he figured, turning pro would have stopped him from playing amateur lacrosse, baseball and hockey. "Canadian football players were considered amateurs," he explained. "Although it was known they took a few dollars. There was no contract. Everything was verbal. Also, I didn't know if I could last in pro football and at that time we had to wait three years before we could regain amateur status."

After his seven-year career with Argonauts he turned to officiating — 12 years in football and nine as a National Hockey League referee. He quit NHL refereeing after a celebrated tiff with NHL President Clarence Campbell. He has nothing but memories of his Dec. 10, 1938, afternoon. "We got rings, but I lost mine. It was wrapped in tissue paper. My sister thought it was just an old piece of paper and tossed it in the kitchen stove fire. My ring went with it."

CHAPTER IX

THE AMERICAN IMPORT FIGHT

Dec. 9, 1939, at Ottawa
Winnipeg Blue Bombers 8, Ottawa Rough Riders 7

Canada was at war again. In Halifax harbor a convoy of Canadian troop ships waited patiently for a sailing tide. The 1st Division had embarked secretly. But not all their thoughts were on the unknown perils of the Atlantic or overseas that awaited them.

They wondered what was happening in the Grey Cup final at Lansdowne Park in Ottawa. The men from the West were betting that the Blue Bombers would again upset the East — just as they did when they won the West's first Cup in 1935. Besides, the Rough Riders had knocked Toronto Argonauts off their pedestal as Big Four champions and the Westerners wouldn't have to contend with the well-known Argo bounce or that pesky Red Storey.

Besides, Coach Reg Threlfall of the Bombers was again in fine voice. No, his Bombers would not cut the Easterners off at the knees as he said his club would do against Argos in 1938. This time, he took another tack. While scouting Riders in the Eastern final he conceded that the Eastern club had the weight advantage along the line, but "we'll erase that with our faster and harder-charging line," he predicted. He was right. And a flash to Halifax told the troops the result — and just how right Threlfall was — before they sailed that night.

Back at Ottawa and with temperatures a chilly 22 above, a yelling mob of 11,738 was witnessing one of the most thrilling Cup games. The state of world affairs hadn't suspended football. On the contrary, service heads saw it as a morale builder and urged its continuance. Later, they were to authorize formation of service teams.

Football had the blessing of everyone — but it couldn't get along with itself. There were rumblings again. East-West differences over United States imports and conflicting East-West playing rules had broken out. Meetings were held. Differences were deep-rooted and only the glib tongue of Joe Ryan, the chain-smoking Winnipeg manager, had saved this year's game. The man who years later was to become general manager of Montreal Alouettes and Edmonton Eskimos and who went out to Victoria in retirement was a convincing Western spokesman at Canadian Rugby Union meetings.

Some people said Ryan would have to do more tall talking to save the classic. This might be the last one unless the West, whose thinking on football matters was far ahead of the East, conformed to the CRU playing rules. The East said linemen could block three yards beyond the line of scrimmage. The West said open up the game, make it 10 yards. The East stuck to the decision and the Bombers, who had played the 10-yard rules throughout the season, switched to the Eastern regulations. One way or another, they vowed, they'd beat the East.

The troops in Halifax and the frozen fans in the stands weren't thinking of this when Bombers and Riders took the field. The rugged battle was tied 6-6 at half-time and the third quarter was scoreless.

The teams traded singles in the fourth quarter. On the first play of the quarter Les Lear — later to coach Calgary in the 1948 Cup thriller over Rough Riders — poured through to block an Ottawa kick. Winnipeg got the ball 10 yards from the Ottawa goal line and Greg Kabat's field goal try was wide and went for a single.

Tiny Hermann tied it 7-7 for the Riders when his placement also was wide and bounced into the end zone for a point. The stage then was set for Orville Burke's most disappointing day. The sure-handed Rough Rider hadn't fumbled a ball all season. He circled under a booming punt by Winnipeg's Art Stevenson and his record suddenly was broken. He dropped the ball, Jeff Nicklin scooped it up for Bombers and ran 10 yards to the Ottawa 35.

With less than a minute to go, Stevenson got away another punt behind the Ottawa goal line. Burke tried to return the kick but the ball struck the side of his foot and slithered out of touch on the Ottawa eight-yard line. Winnipeg's ball, the seconds ticking off and Bombers again lined up in punt formation. Stevenson, a 21-year-old 185-pounder who had gone to Bombers this year from Hastings College, Nebraska, made no mistake on this one. He booted it into the end-zone crowd for the game-winning point. The West had won its second Grey Cup. Men in uniform spilled onto the field and mauled the happy Westerners.

Nicklin, who had been an important man in the victory, was to lose his life in France on March 24, 1945. Officers and men of his paratroop battalion donated a trophy in his memory and the Jeff Nicklin Memorial Trophy is still awarded each year to the player in the Western Conference judged most valuable to his team.

And little Fritzie Hanson, the Winnipeg flash who almost single-handedly won the Cup game in 1935, announced his retirement. But Fritzie wasn't through. Football fans were to see him again in 1948 when Calgary Stampeders whipped Ottawa 12-7 in a tremendous upset. The Bombers took the Cup for another train ride in 1939 and, again, the trophy returned alone the next year. The committee room infighting had broken out again and the West was out in the cold while a couple of Eastern clubs battled for the trophy.

There would be a day, vowed Westerners, when they would have equal power with the East in this business of operating football on a national scale. It took a long, long time and the rewards were worth it when Edmonton Eskimos, then the Bombers, made it abundantly clear that, come Grey Cup Day, it could meet the East on equal terms. And win.

CHAPTER X

THE GREAT RULE BATTLE

The Early Forties

The Canadian Rugby Union acted like a petulant, stubborn school-master. Reg Threlfall won another Grey Cup for Winnipeg with a rambunctious old pro who had decided to learn the art of field goal kicking. Lew Hayman had a vision and won the trophy for the fourth time and bookmakers proved they were mere mortals by install-ing the West as favorites to win the Cup the year that Joe Krol loped onto the national football scene.

These unrelated string of curcumstances started in 1940, the year that the CRU scolded the West, specifically Winnipeg Blue Bombers, and told them there would be no East-West final because they did not play the game according to the rule book as they had been told to do in 1938.

It compounded this error by staging an unprecendented two-game, total-point series involving Toronto Balmy Beach, Ontario Rugby Football Union champion, and Ottawa Rough Riders, Big Four title-holders. With this bombshell, it appeared for a time that a part of the big war in Europe had been transferred to Canada.

Western officials tried a let's-be-reasonable approach. It didn't work. They then cajoled and threatened. Nothing doing, said the CRU. The Sports Service League suggested what it considered a sure-fire solu-tion. It proposed an East-West final on Saturday, Dec. 7, with net proceeds to go for sports equipment for Canadian troops overseas.

The Bombers agreed. So did Beaches, if they got past the Rough Riders in the Eastern final. Rough Riders gave lip service, saying that would be fine if the CRU sanctioned the contest. It didn't come because the powers in the East voted against the proposal. The total-point series was arranged.

Rough Riders won the first game 8-2 on Nov. 30 at Varsity Stadium in Toronto on a bitterly cold afternoon. Only 4,993 fans turned out and receipts were $3,925.50. A week later at Lansdowne Park in Ottawa, the smallest crowd in Cup history — 1,700 — watched the Riders win the game 12-5 and the round 20-7. Gate receipts were a mere $1,798, also the smallest since the Cup was put up for competition in 1909.

Ironically, the date of the second game, Dec. 7, was to be the proposed date for the charity contest. Tempers flared and action was fast. On Dec. 13, an angry West pulled out of the CRU. Two days later, James Bannerman of Calgary, CRU president, resigned. And on Dec. 17, the CRU declared Ottawa Rough Riders the 1940 Cup champions — 10 days after the final. "Cheese champions and two-bit operators," growled disgusted Westerners. They were repeating the words of Al Ritchie of Regina Roughriders in 1936 when his Western champions were booted out of Cup contention over the question of U.S. imports.

But early in 1941 football men in the West decided that compromise was the only solution. They gave up the rule providing for blocking by linemen 10 yards beyond the line of scrimmage, which it had been told to do in 1938. In return, the East grudgingly extended its three-yard regulation to five yards. It was a backward step for football. The West had been trying for years to open up the game and make it more exciting for the spectators. But, it reasoned, it would have to go along with the rule-makers if it expected to challenge for the Cup.

Differences were patched up and the West proved three points: It could adapt to Eastern rules, get the crowds back into the park for the big game, and win. But other drastic changes were still to be made in both the East and West. On July 24, 1941, the Interprovincial Rugby Football Union, popularly known as the Big Four, was dissolved when Hamilton Tigers folded. Toronto Balmy Beach was admitted to the newly-formed Eastern Canada Rugby Football Union, but the league never did get off the ground.

There was no league play. Instead, a two-game total-point series was scheduled with Ottawa meeting Toronto Argonauts and the winner advancing to the Cup final against the Western champions. Ottawa won 18-17 on the round. But the West also had problems. Calgary Bronks had folded, leaving only Winnipeg and Regina in the

The Right Hon. Earl Grey, G.C.M.G. Incoming Governor-General of Canada, 1904 and donor of the Grey Cup — football's most prized trophy.

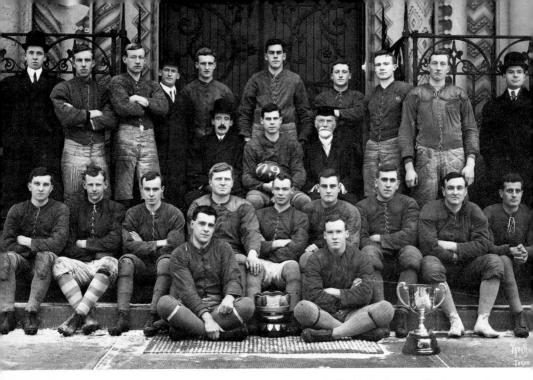

University of Toronto Senior Rugby Football Club. Intercollegiate and Dominion Champions 1909. The first official Grey Cup winners.

Hughie Gall, one of the all-time great punters in Canadian football who could kick with either foot, shows the punting style of the pre-First World War years that brought him fame with the University of Toronto Blues — first Grey Cup winners in 1909.

The present-day heavy armor, face guards and other protective bric-a-brac weren't even heard about in 1909. Here, Ottawa Rough Riders in white and University of Toronto are all tangled up in the 1909 Grey Cup semi-final at Toronto. Varsity won 31-7 and easily beat Toronto Parkdale 26-6 in the final.

Carriages line up along the sidelines to watch the 1910 Grey Cup semi-final between the University of Toronto and the Toronto Amateur Athletic Club at Rosedale field. Varsity won.

Halfback Jack Maynard of the University of Toronto attempts a difficult goal in the 1910 Grey Cup final while Hughie Gall, great kicking half of the Blues holds the ball.

Harry Batstone (left) and Pep Leadlay (right) played on the mighty Queen's University Grey Cup championship teams in 1922-23-24. Batstone joined the Kingston, Ontario University from the Toronto Argonauts, 1921 Grey Cup champions.

Crew-cut Lionel Conacher succeeded Smirle Lawson as football's "Big Train". Conacher, who died in 1954, was voted the outstanding athlete of the half century in a 1950 poll conducted by the Canadian Press. He played with Toronto Argonauts in the first East-West final in 1921 when they beat the Edmonton Eskimos 23-0.

Respected and widely-read Toronto Telegram sports columnist, and member of football's Hall of Fame, Ted Reeve has always held a warm spot in his big heart for the men on the line. Here he is as a member of the 1930 Toronto Balmy Beach Cup-winning team. He was one of the men in the pit.

Warren Stevens (left) threw it and Kenny Grant (right) caught it. The "it" was the first Cup touchdown pass in 1931 when Montreal Winged Wheelers shut out Regina Roughriders 22-0 at Montreal. The historic pass, a 40-yarder, was completed in the third quarter of the game.

Alexandra Studios

Fritz Hanson, speedy backfielder with Winnipeg Blue Bombers, galloped through the mud at Hamilton in one of the most spectacular one-man performances in Grey Cup history. On Dec. 7, 1935, Winnipeg and Hanson gave the West its first Cup victory, an 18-12 decision over the heavily favored Hamilton Tigers.

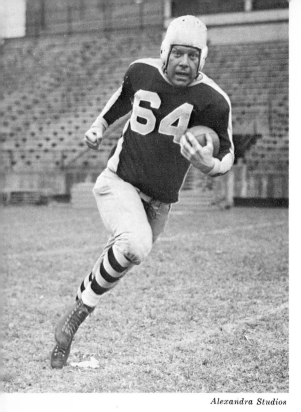

As a young sprite in Barrie, Ontario, Red Storey was overshadowed by his tom-boyish sister, Irene, on a team known as the "Tiffin Street Terrors." He sprouted to a brawny 6'-3" 200-pounder, joined the Toronto Argonauts and in the final quarter of the 1938 Cup final, scored three touchdowns as the Argos defeated the Winnipeg Blue Bombers 30-7.

Alexandra Studios

Gravel-voiced Teddy Morris, always a staunch believer in Canadian football players, coached Toronto Argonauts to three straight Cup titles with all-Canadian teams. He played with Argo Cup-winning clubs in 1933, 1936 and 1937, and piloted the Double Blues to national championships over the Winnipeg Blue Bombers in 1945, 1946 and 1947.

Alexandra Studios

league. Vancouver Grizzlies were invited to play with the Blue Bombers and Roughriders.

The Grizzlies, coached by Greg Kabat of Blue Bomber fame, won one of eight league games, scored a total of only 15 points while yielding 109. Blue Bombers topped the league and then defeated Regina in the best-of-three final. And so east came Winnipeg's Reg Threlfall, a colorful character of many talents, talking all the way. He forecast that a few Ottawa heads would bounce around the Varsity Stadium turf and he could see no reason why Bombers couldn't make it two straight over the Rough Riders. He recalled Winnipeg's 8-7 victory over Riders in 1939 at Ottawa.

Many of the 1939 Bombers and Ottawa players were back for the rematch. But missing from the Winnipeg lineup was Art Stevenson, who had kicked a single into the end zone crowd in the final seconds of the 1939 game to win the contest. He was injured but Threlfall still boasted that his club was the best.

The teams took the field on Nov. 29 in 58-degree weather and with a sellout Cup record crowd of 19,065 in the stands. Gate receipts were $17,592.75, a handsome figure in these days, and a record. The grin on Threlfall's face after the game ended was as wide as his floppy fedora. Bombers won 18-16 in a thriller that could easily have gone into overtime. Only 12 inches separated the Riders from a tie in regulation time.

In the last minutes of the game George Fraser, Ottawa's giant middle and placement-kicking specialist, tried a field goal from 18 yards out, with Bombers ahead 18-15. He watched in despair as the ball sailed wide by a foot and rolled to the deadline for a single.

But Fraser wasn't the goat in this game. He had previously kicked three field goals — from the 16-, 28- and 17-yard lines and had converted an unorthodox and sensational touchdown by Tony Golab, Ottawa's bright young star known as the Golden Boy who was to have a distinguished career with Riders.

Golab's touchdown was of a kind never seen before, or again, in a Cup final. In the first quarter he punted high and short, evaded his block, and took his own kick on the Winnipeg 45-yard line. No one laid a hand on him as he raced all the way into the Bomber end zone. Fraser's three placements were a single-game Cup record.

But the hero of the game was Ches McCance, acting captain of the Bombers. He was a happy-go-lucky player who made road trips

73

one long laugh for teammates. The old-time Bomber crowd remember him best as a fun-loving man who was the despair of coaches off the field.

Few of the fans, executives or players who travelled around the West during league games or East for the Grey Cup will forget Ches frying bacon and eggs in a Pullman car or walking barefoot through a diner, dipping his toe into a passenger's coffee, then shouting to the waiter: "Bring this man another cup of coffee. This one's cold."

But with the pads on he was a no-nonsense individual. In 1941 he had been around football a few years, and that season, for the first time, he tried kicking field goals and found that he could master the art. In the Cup final he kicked two placements — his second a 38-yarder in the third quarter that broke a 15-15 tie. His first effort, from 24 yards out in the opening quarter, put Bombers ahead 3-0. He later kicked the converts on touchdowns by Mel Wilson and Bud Marquardt.

Big Ches, who loved life and everybody in it, was a natural athlete. After a stint in the armed services during the Second World War he moved to Montreal where he joined the Alouettes under Lew Hayman. He returned to Winnipeg a few years after his retirement from football following the 1949 Grey Cup game during which he contributed seven points to Als' 28-15 victory over Calgary Stampeders.

As a basketball player, he starred with Winnipeg St. Andrew's in many bids for Canadian championships. He was twice a member of Quebec rinks in the Canadian curling championship. And he was a better-than-average soccer and lacrosse player. Ches died in his sleep in his Winnipeg home on May 8, 1956, at the age of 40.

In that 1941 Grey Cup game the Bombers had Fritzie Hanson, Mel Wilson, Les Lear, Cliff Roseborough, Lou Mogul, Jack Manners, Bernie Thornton, Nat Shore, Benny Hatskin, Ken Draper, Herb Peschel, Rube Ludwig, Ken Preston, Wayne Sheley, Jim Lander, Art Kolisnyk, Larry Boivin, Kip McFadyen, Wilf Daniels, Lloyd Evenson, Chick Chikowski and Jim Hutchison.

With Ottawa were Andy Tommy, Tommy Daley, Murray Griffin, Orville Burke, George Fraser, Curly Moynahan, Leo Seguin, Paul McGarry, Dave Sprague, Tony McCarthy, Bunny Wadsworth, Pete O'Connor, Tim Langley, Jack Taylor, Bert Haigh, Bill Klimenko, Eric Chipper, Stan O'Neil, Arnie McWatters, Arnie Charbonneau, Johnny Fripp, Wilf Tremblay, Fred Syms. The coach was Ross Trimble.

After this game, the third triumph for the West and all by Winnipeg teams, and the second for Threlfall, more changes were made in the game. The one-year-old Eastern Canada Rugby Football Union folded in August, 1941. Armed forces teams took over and ready to enter the picture was Lew Hayman, the Syracuse kid who had coached Toronto Argonaut teams to Cup titles in 1933-1937-1938.

One day early in 1942, Hayman walked into the office of Squadron Leader E. W. (Ted) Kenrick at No. 1 Training School in Toronto and made a flat prediction: "We've got a Grey Cup team at the station." "Sure we have," mumbled Squadron Leader Kenrick, who later became a magistrate at Haileybury, Ont., "and we've also got a war on." He looked up from the pile of papers on his desk and nearly flipped. The visitor was Flying Officer Lew Hayman, a chap who would have to wipe the perspiration off his brow in a heat wave to agree it was a warm day.

Lew had worried and fretted through nine seasons as coach of Argonauts and here he was out of civvies, and out of character. Hayman had spotted at the air station such familiar football figures as Fred Kijek, Don Durno, Cece Foderingham, Joey Richman, George Oliphant, Jake Gaudaur, Eddie Berton, Bill Stukus, Art West, Eddie Thompson, Jack Buckmaster, Truck Langley, John (Pop) Poplowsky. Another was Jack Parry, a speedster who later competed for Canada in track in the 1948 Summer Olympic Games at London.

Kenrick reported to Air Chief Marshal Lloyd S. Breadner, who gave the go-ahead but stressed that the project must not interfere with the station's training program. Lew had the bodies but no equipment and Hamilton Tigers told him to help himself with their gear but warned that it would have to be returned if the war ended suddenly and the league resumed operations.

Hayman got a franchise for the newly-formed Toronto RCAF-Hurricanes in the Ontario Rugby Football Union and proceeded to run away from the opposition. Hurricanes ended the 10-game schedule with eight victories, a tie and a loss, shut out Balmy Beach 24-0 in the sudden-death final and beat Ottawa Uplands 18-13 in the Eastern final.

They were ready for Winnipeg RCAF-Bombers and Threlfall once again. But there was trouble again. Headquarters in Ottawa said that air force teams would not be permitted to play after Dec. 1 and the Cup final had been set for Dec. 12. Fortunately, Air Marshal

Breadner was able to solve the problem easily by setting a Dec. 5 deadline and the clubs met it.

Once again Threlfall was telling anyone and everyone what was wrong with the East. This year he picked on the defences. Teams in the East, he said, "use the same defensive formation on Dec. 5 that they used on Sept. 5." Hayman said nothing. He was too busy worrying. Threlfall's assessment was right on the button up to half time when Hurricanes led by a scant 2-0 margin. Hurricanes had been bothered by short Winnipeg passes and it appeared at times that the Bombers would suddenly break through and go all the way.

During the half-time intermission, Hayman made a switch in his defences. He ordered his outsides to charge the Bomber ends, hoping this would prevent would-be receivers on short passes from getting to the ball in time. It worked and the West, which had only a sputtering ground attack, lost its only worthwhile offensive. Hurricanes won 8-5.

"It was the last truly amateur team to win the Cup," said Hurricanes' Don Durno at a team reunion in 1962. "My payoff was $15, two pounds of butter and a pound of tea." Lew Hayman was at the reunion. And not very happy. He was back with Argonauts and, for the 10th consecutive year, they were Cup spectators.

In 1943 Joe Krol, probably the greatest money player Canadian football has known, and Hamilton Flying Wildcats won the East with one-time Hamilton Tiger great Brian Timmis as coach. Back again were the RCAF-Bombers from Winnipeg and Threlfall. This was the year when the Eastern bookmakers and their senses parted company. They installed Winnipeg 8-to-5 favorites. Maybe they were mesmerized by the fast-talking Threlfall or maybe they calculated that Krol had run out of steam. It was a reasonable supposition because Threlfall had a fine team. But it was a mistake to bet against Krol, a triple threat and a player who had a knack of waiting for the final minutes to come up with the big plays that won games.

He had already shown that ability on Nov. 20, just one week before the Cup final, when he spearheaded a final-minute 85-yard touchdown drive to beat Lachine RCAF 8-7 in the sudden-death Eastern final. He had been pretty much of a bust for the first 57 minutes of that game. He had scored a second-quarter single that put Wildcats in front 1-0 but Lachine went ahead 6-1 in the third quarter on a converted touchdown. Krol moved Hurricanes downfield with his passing and kicked the game winning point with his convert of a three-yard touchdown by Paul Peterson.

Against this background, and the fact that Wildcats were considered lucky to beat the Quebec champions, the bookies gambled that Krol couldn't do it again in the East-West final. The RCAF-Bombers had beaten Regina All Services 1-0 and 11-0 and again with many of the players who had won the Cup in 1939 and 1941 — Les Lear, McCance and Rube Ludwig among them. But they lost 23-14 in the Cup on Saturday, Nov. 27, with a crowd of 16,423 looking on at Varsity Stadium.

The Westerners beat the Wildcats everywhere but on the scoreboard. Bombers made 11 first downs to five for Hamilton. They gained 250 yards from scrimmage — 199 yards rushing and 51 on passing. Hamilton gained 165 yards, 126 on the ground and 39 in the air.

Krol threw a touchdown pass to Doug Smith in the opening minutes and then added seven points of his own on three converts, a single and a field goal. Wildcats really won the game with an 18-7 first-quarter blitz and held off the desperate Bombers in the remaining 45 minutes.

Back in Winnipeg after the game, the RCAF-Bombers were welcomed as heroes by Lieutenant-Governor R. F. McWilliams, Premier Stuart Garson of Manitoba, civic, army and air force brass and hundreds of football fans. Threlfall did not disappoint them.

"The Hamilton team, no doubt, knew they had been in a ball game and not a yo-yo contest," he said. "What's more, I really believe if our boys were to meet that same Hamilton team again they would win four out of five times." But, sadly, it was the end of the line as a football coach for the 40-year-old graduate of Purdue University. He resigned because of pressure of business as an insurance executive.

"A successful job in football requires a lot of time and I can't see myself with that kind of time to spare," he said. His resignation was a blow to Winnipeg, and to football generally in Canada. Since hitting Winnipeg in 1938 he led Blue Bomber and RCAF-Bomber teams to six Western Canada titles, competed in five Cup finals and won two. He had added color and excitement to the game and knew how to attract the crowds, even in wartime when the people of Canada had their minds more on Canadians in uniform overseas than on football players.

In 1944, the West did not have football and, for the last time, the

Cup was an all-Eastern contest. It was played in Hamilton and Montreal HMCS Donnaconas defeated the Flying Wildcats 7-6 before a crowd of only 3,871 who paid $3,425 at the gate.

Krol was back with the Wildcats, this time coached by Glen Brown. It became the only Cup loss in Krol's sparkling career. As usual, though, he provided some last-minute heroics by driving Wildcats to a touchdown that, with Krol's convert, tied the score at 6-6. Dutch Davey, who later went to Sarnia Imperials, kicked the winning point for Montreal.

The war ended the next year and football painstakingly returned to normal. Winnipeg and Regina decided to field teams in 1945 and play some exhibition games, followed by a playoff to decide which club would go into the East-West final. Calgary spoiled that plan by organizing the Stampeders club. Meanwhile, in the East, Lew Hayman went from Toronto to Montreal to coach the Big Four club known as the Hornets, and Argos hired Teddy Morris as coach. Argos also got Krol from Hamilton and a backfield sidekick known as Royal Copeland. Argonaut fans would never forget this threesome. Neither would Winnipeg Blue Bombers.

CHAPTER XI

ARGOS AND TEDDY MORRIS

Dec. 1, 1945, at Toronto
Toronto Argonauts 35, Winnipeg Blue Bombers 0

Teddy Morris was an angry young man. So infuriated, in fact, he accepted the job of coaching Toronto Argonauts. It is one of those improbable, but believable, stories about people involved in the Grey Cup. One summer day this year, Teddy was called into the office of Argo president Tommy Alison and for nearly 15 minutes the usually-placid little man sizzled while Alison was on the telephone.

Teddy recalled the incident in 1964, just one year before his untimely death in Toronto at the age of 55. "When I arrived in Mr. Alison's office he was on the phone with a club director. He kept repeating 'but Teddy's all we've got to fall back on.' I kept interrupting to say 'now, just a gosh-danged minute,' but Mr. Alison kept repeating that line.

"I got mad because nobody has ever had to apologize for me for anything in my life. They needed a coach and I guess somebody happened to think of me. Lew Hayman had gone to coach Montreal Hornets and Argos were stuck." During Alison's phone conversation, Teddy was mulling over in his mind whether he should walk out on the club that he had been so closely associated with as a player for more than a decade. But he accepted the job to prove a few things to the Argonaut doubters. That, undoubtedly, was the most satisfactory move that Argos—and Teddy—had ever made. The little man with the cowlick and the gravel voice was an instant success.

Many people, including Frank Clair who took over from Teddy in 1950 and who went on to become one of the most successful coaches in Canadian pro football, owe a lot to that down-to-earth man who believed until his death that the Canadian player, given the chance, could hold his own against any American.

With all-Canadian lineups he laid the foundation for the most productive era in the history of any club in Canada—five Cup championship teams in eight years. Before he left the scene after the 1949 season when clubs started scrambling for American coaches and players, Teddy had brought Argonauts to three straight national titles. He sat in the stands in 1950 and 1952 when Argo teams made up mostly of players he had tutored and were now coached by Clair, won the Cup.

The year 1945 was one of fond memories for Toronto football fans. Teddy was in his freshman year as coach. Across town, Ted Reeve was back from the war as a member of Conn Smythe's Sportsmen's Battery. Gunner Reeve had been hit by what he called a "flying rock" during a German artillery barrage in France. It had happened near Caen in July and it took him until Nov. 4 to mention that his left elbow had hurt him "some". His elbow was found to be fractured and army doctors decided to send him back home where he closed out a great career; first as a player with Toronto Balmy Beach of the ORFU for the prior 15 years, and this year as honorary coach of his beloved Beaches.

Reeve arrived back in Canada with his arm in a sling. Anyone who asked him what happened the Gunner merely replied "I finally ran out of tape." That was a reference to his playing days when yards of the stuff were needed to keep him in one piece.

With that he went back to the game he loved. Beaches had won the ORFU title, Argonauts the Big Four. Beach players knew that this was to be Ted's farewell to the game and, as a mark of respect and admiration, they wanted to present him with the Eastern title and a shot at Winnipeg Blue Bombers in the Cup final. But Argos were too powerful.

Morris, the only man the club had to "fall back on" in the summer, had built a blockbuster—the gold-dust twins of Krol and Royal Copeland, hardrocks Bill Zock, Frankie Morris, Les Ascott, John and Steve Levantis, Tommy Glenn, Don Loney, Pat Santucci, Roy Smylie, Murray and Pete Titanic, Tom Walden, Jack Wedley, Art West, Byron and Steve Karrys, Fred Doty, Leo Deadey, Chuck Camilleri, Pete Carr-Harris, Len Cassidy, Billy Myers, Billy Neale, Jimmy O'Brien, Steve Pruski, Pat Reid, Bernie Richardson, Don Robinson, Art Skidmore, Murray (Red) Sullivan and Boris Tipoff.

Argos beat the Beaches 14-2 before a crowd of 18,600. Among the spectators was Bert Warwick, Winnipeg coach, and the Argonaut performance undoubtedly convinced him that it would be a long afternoon for the Western champions the following Saturday. It was. All the way over a sticky, snow-sheathed Varsity Stadium field where Argonauts had beaten Blue Bomber teams in 1937 and 1938, it was a case of running and passing power erupting against demoralized Bomber defenders.

Billy Myers, a 135-pounder, and Doug Smylie, a 155-pounder, each scored a pair of touchdowns. At quarterback was Fred Doty. Krol and Copeland added one touchdown each and Krol tossed a couple of touchdown passes after taking pitchouts and added a pair of converts. Art Skidmore kicked a single.

It was a heartbreaker for the Bombers, but they had nothing to be ashamed about. Football was confined more or less to the schools in the West and the WIFU had operated as a two-team league—Winnipeg and Regina—until Calgary Stampeders entered the picture late in the season. And Winnipeg had played some exhibition games against American teams under U.S. rules before going East. Calgary pulled a big surprise with 3-1 and 12-0 victories over Regina but, in the final, lost 9-6 to the Bombers.

The Bombers, with Ches McCance, Lloyd Boivin, Nat Shore, Mel Wilson, Bert Iannone, Jack Manners, Rube Ludwig and a few other veterans in the lineup, only once showed signs in the Grey Cup contest of the strength that won the Western title. That brief moment came late in the game when they moved along the ground for three straight first downs to the Argonaut 10-yard line. But young Harry Hood fumbled on a line play and Toronto recovered the ball to erase the last threat in the game.

It was a sweet victory for Morris, who had never received more than $500 a season as a player and who was paid $5,000 a year as coach. He saved his money to buy a couple of farms in the vicinity of what later became known as Toronto International Airport, worked the land himself and sold 100 acres to the federal government for a sum well into six figures. He still had another 100 acres at the time of his death. As the man said: "Nobody has ever had to apologize for me for anything in my life."

CHAPTER XII

EAST-WEST LOVE AFFAIR

Nov. 30, 1946, at Toronto
Toronto Argonauts 28, Winnipeg Blue Bombers 6

The Canadian Rugby Union bowed to what it termed "popular demand" and adopted the 10-yard blocking rule for linemen. Not only that, the CRU told its affiliated unions to go ahead and play five imports a team if they wished, with no strings attached.

Amen, said Western football officials who had been campaigning for relaxed playing rule and import regulations for years. Ahem, coughed Easterners on the CRU rules committee, who acted as if they had known all along that the double-barrelled legislation was their brainchild.

The historic decisions were taken at a meeting in Toronto on Feb. 13 that year and they wiped out long-standing East-West differences. The West had pleaded for an easing of import regulations since the early 1930s and had been rebuffed. The West had adopted the 10-yard interference rule in its own conference in 1937, had asked the CRU to make this standard across the country and the East-dominated CRU said no.

The West had been kicked out of a berth in the 1936 Grey Cup final because of blurred residence rules concerning imports imposed by the CRU. It had been kicked out of the 1940 Cup final because it had not adhered to the East's five-yard blocking rule. The East had made a couple of concessions in the late 1930s and early 1940s regarding the playing rules. For instance, it extended its blocking by linesmen to five yards from three yards. The West had introduced the forward pass into Canada in 1929 and the CRU grudgingly said it was okay, but ruled that a pass could not be thrown from inside the defensive team's 25-yard line. Finally, in 1936, it went all the way and said the pass could be thrown from anywhere on the field. And now, in 1946, the CRU reached the conclusion that the West had been right after all.

The forward pass and the extended blocking made for more exciting football games. But the limit of five Americans for East and West did not catch on immediately.

Western clubs had some financial problems and only two, Saskatchewan Roughriders and Winnipeg Blue Bombers, brought in Americans. The Roughriders imported three and Bombers four. Ottawa Rough Riders of the Eastern Big Four went the limit—five. Montreal, now known as the Alouettes with Lew Hayman, sports promoter Leo Dandurand and Toronto stockbroker Eric Cradock as co-owners, brought in six, including Herb Trawick who was to remain for a decade. Hayman explained he wanted to take a good look before cutting the extra man.

Fan reaction? A survey by The Canadian Press showed that more than half a million spectators—an all-time record to this point—watched games in eight Canadian cities. Montreal Als set a single-game attendance record with 22,000 fans who paid $45,000 when Als were eliminated by the all-Canadian Toronto Argonauts in the Big Four final.

Canadian coaches, in the main, decided they could do without the Americans until the Calgary Stampeders travelled East in 1948 with several Americans and beat Ottawa Rough Riders. Only then did other Canadian teams decide it was time to go the limit. But 1946 was a vintage year for the East, and coach Teddy Morris of Argonauts.

A crowd of 18,960 paid their way into Varsity Stadium for the Argo-Blue Bomber game. Argonauts piled up a 28-0 lead and were headed for a shutout until the final minute when quarterback Wally Dobler, a newcomer from North Dakota, scored a Winnipeg touchdown from the Toronto three-yard line and kicked the convert himself.

Joe Krol pitched three touchdown srikes for Toronto—to Royal Copeland, Doug Smylie and Boris Tipoff. Krol also kicked three converts and caught a touchdown pass from Copeland. In addition, Krol lofted an onside kick that Copeland caught just short of the goal line and Byron Karrys carried over on the next play.

Krol to Copeland, Copeland to Krol. It was getting monotonous and coach Jack West of the Bombers was the first to admit it. "When you've got a receiver like Copeland, and a passer like Krol, and he's having a good day—well, it's a lot of touchdowns, that's all there is to it," he said.

It was touch and go whether the teams played out the clock. After Winnipeg's touchdown in the game's final seconds, Chuck Camerilli took the kickoff and high-tailed it for the Argonaut bench where he presented the game ball to Coach Teddy Morris, a little man in rumpled old trousers, grey shirt and a shock of black hair covering most of his forehead.

CHAPTER XIII

JOE KING KROL

Nov. 29, 1947, at Toronto
Toronto Argonauts 10, Winnipeg Blue Bombers 9

Take your .400 hitters in baseball, 50-goal National Hockey League scorers, back-nine final-round chargers in golf such as Arnold Palmer and you have a composite of Joe Krol, football player.

Make a mistake and he would kill you. Give him the eye of a needle to shoot at and he would thread it with a football.

In 1946 Jack Manners of Winnipeg Blue Bombers said after Argos and Krol beat the Western champions 28-6 in the Cup final, "I'm afraid we'll be old men before we beat Argos and Krol."

It didn't matter whether Krol was the quarterback or a lonely figure sitting on the end of the bench who stretched his legs only to punt, Argos won the big ones with him on the roster. Argos and Krol met Winnipeg again in 1950 and the game ended 13-0 for Argos. They beat Edmonton Eskimos in 1952 by a 21-11 score.

No player in the game except, possibly, Jackie Parker of Edmonton Eskimos and Russ Jackson of Ottawa Rough Riders could do what Krol could. Parker could win a game with a long run, as he proved in 1954 with a late-game touchdown gallop against Edmonton. Jackson could do it with his forward passing or his running.

Krol did it with his throwing, running, catching and kicking. He had done it time and again in games that counted and the 1947 Cup final was no exception for the 28-year-old native of Windsor, Ont. He kicked Argonauts' opening point. He threw a touchdown pass to Royal Copeland, converted it and added another four singles to take a hand in all Argo scoring.

The 18,885 fans at Varsity Stadium who watched the action on a hard, fast field probably never will forget Krol's performance, climaxed when he kicked the winning point. The ball landed as the final whistle blew following a Blue Bomber gamble in Winnipeg territory that didn't pay off. Bob Sandberg, a 210-pound quarterback from the University of Minnesota who did everything for the Bombers—punt, pass and plunge—decided with only seconds remaining on a play that failed. He lost the ball on downs to Argos just when the game appeared headed for the first overtime session in Cup history.

On third down with the score tied 9-9 and Bombers in punt formation, Sandberg handed off to Bert Iannone who was stopped at the line of scrimmage. With play on the Winnipeg 33-yard line, Krol punted to the deadline for the winning point. Coach Jack West of Bombers disagreed with the second-guessers that Sandberg had made a mistake. "Sandberg realized that if the game went into overtime we would be no match for Argos' powerful reserve strength. It would just be postponing the inevitable. That play worked for us before and it may have worked this time for a long gain," he said after the game.

It was a big victory for Argos. They had trailed 9-0 well into the second quarter after a four-yard touchdown plunge by Sandberg, a convert by Don Hiney and a field goal by Hiney. Shortly before halftime Krol kicked a single. In the third quarter Frankie Morris of Argos picked up a fumble by Harry Hood on the Winnipeg 38. On the next play Krol hit Copeland with a TD pass, converted it and Bombers' lead was cut to 9-7.

With five minutes remaining in the game, Argonauts three times drove into range for Krol to kick single points. Bombers might have climbed out of reach on one play early in the fourth quarter. It was a fake placement from the Argo 35 with Sandberg holding the ball for Hiney. Sandberg threw a pass to Johnny Reagan instead. The slender half raced all the way for a touchdown but it was called back when officials ruled the forward had not crossed the scrimmage line.

The arguments over that play will never be settled to everyone's satisfaction. Reagan said he was sure he caught the pass beyond the line of scrimmage, linesman Bill Rogin and umpire Hec Crighton, both of Toronto, said it was a good two yards shy.

Four days later, they replayed the game in Technicolor, but the movies didn't show the full play. The cameraman forgot to keep his eye on the ball. The movies showed the ball snapped to Sandberg. Hiney went through the motions of kicking a placement while Sandberg straightened up with the ball and dodged behind him. All this time, Reagan was blocking four yards behind the line of scrimmage. Sandberg started to raise his arm with the ball. Reagan appeared to be moving forward and the next picture showed a perfect view of the Argo goal-posts as the camera swung to follow what the cameraman thought was a placement kick.

By the time the camera swung back to the play, Reagan was at about the Argo 15-yard line. This scene also showed Crighton marking the spot where the ball was caught, a good two yards behind the line of scrimmage.

This was the only complete movie record of the game. Another movie company took pictures but officials said they had edited the disputed play out of their version because it wasn't a scoring play.

It was a bitter defeat for the Westerners who played well enough to win. They gained 210 yards on the ground against 172 for Argonauts, completed four of eight passes for 91 yards against three of six for 39 yards by Argos.

Argos celebrated with a party, but coach Teddy Morris wasn't around. He had hurried home after the game to nurse a sick horse on his farm just outside Toronto.

CHAPTER XIV

THE LAST SLEEPER PLAY

Nov. 27, 1948, at Toronto
Calgary Stampeders 12, Ottawa Rough Riders 7

Was this a con job? A three-man piece of chicanery? "Why," said Coach Les Lear of the Stampeders, "hell, no." "Unh-unh," said halfback Normie Hill. "Naw," said quarterback Keith Spaith. "We didn't even think about it."

The "it" was Calgary's sleeper-play touchdown that sent the Stamps winging to a fantastic Cup triumph and that sent football itself into a boom era unmatched by any sport in the country.

Spaith threw the pass. Hill caught it. And Lear engineered it. One must take the pious word of the three principals that this play just happened, but when all the pieces are put into place, suspicion points up to the most dazzling snow job in the history of the trophy.

On Friday morning, about 28 hours before the Cup kickoff, Lear was driven from the Pig 'n Whistle, a highway dine-and-dance spot where the Stampeders were staying, for a 35-mile ride to the Royal York Hotel in Toronto for what he described as "a meeting." He had a few things to straighten out with the Canadian Rugby Union, he said.

Topping the list was his demand that game officials would be instructed in clear, concise language that Rough Rider and Stampeder players would not be allowed to stand near the sidelines while waiting to go into play. The 30-year-old freshman coach did not want to take any chances of Ottawa pulling the sleeper play in such an important contest.

He pointed out that this was the biggest game of the year, that Calgary had waited 37 years for the chance to represent the West and he did not want any bush-league tactics from the Riders. CRU officials agreed and game officials were given their instructions. Lear mentioned that the Rough Riders had pulled the sleeper play several times during the season after substitutions and that Rider players were "always cluttering up the sidelines."

As it turned out every Rough Rider and Stampeder player not on the playing field, plus the water boys, the trainers, coaches, assistant coaches, cheer leaders and members of the band in attendance could have been strung out along the sidelines when Stampeders pulled the play.

It happened on the far side of the field, the farthest point from the benches. It was so unexpected that Rough Rider players didn't know what had hit them. Lear denied that he planned it. In the second quarter, Spaith called an extension play. Hill kept running until he reached the sidelines and flopped to the field. Just about everyone in the 20,013 crowd at Varsity Stadium screamed, hollered and pointed to Hill. But the warnings of Ottawa supporters did not reach Rider players.

Stampeders lined up fast, Spaith faked a pass to the right, drawing Ottawa and Calgary players away from Hill. Then Spaith wheeled and sent a long, hang-up pass to Hill who had scrambled to his feet and dashed to within five yards of the Ottawa line as a couple of suddenly-awake Riders ran in his direction.

Too late. Hill took the pass on the goal line, bobbled the ball briefly as an Ottawa player made a desperate grab at him, gathered the ball back into his arms and fell. The Cup's only sleeper play touchdown had been scored. In 1961, football officials banned the play. With the convert, the Stampeders took the lead and then fell behind 7-6 in the third quarter when Bob Paffrath, quarterback of the Riders, scored a touchdown.

The highly-favored Riders had the best of play and, in the fourth quarter, it appeared that it would be only a matter of time until they crossed the Calgary line and put the game out of reach of the Stampeders. They then pulled one of the Cup's most celebrated miscues.

Paffrath tossed a lateral to Pete Karpuk who fumbled the ball on the Rider 40 and, because it was offside, a horn was sounded to denote a rule infraction, but not a halt to play. Karpuk and other Ottawa players hesitated over the ball.

Rangy Woody Strode of the Stamps, who later became a professional wrestler and movie actor, ambled over to see what it was all about. Following him was centre Chuck Anderson who told Woody to "pick it up and run like hell." Strode grabbed the ball, loped down the field believing he would be called back, and lateralled to Jim Mitchener when Rider tacklers caught up to him. Mitchener ran to the Ottawa 10. On the next play Pete Thodos went over for a touchdown through the unsettled Ottawa line.

That was the game for Lear, his old pros and kids who had whipped undefeated through the Western Conference, were held to a 4-4 tie by Saskatchewan Roughriders in the opening game of the two-game total-point Western playoffs and then made it to Toronto with a 17-6 decision.

The gate receipts for this 1948 game totalled $26,655 and tickets sold for $1 and $1.50, a small ante compared with what was coming. But Lear was not concerned with the future when he brought his players to Toronto. En route to the stadium a couple of hours before the kickoff, he said: "If my kids get nervous before that big crowd up there I'm gonna go in, pat 'em on the buttocks and maybe stick around for a couple of plays. Just to settle 'em down."

Everything worked for the squat 5-11, 228-pound lineman who played guard on offence and corner linebacker on defence. His kids got the jitters early, he went into the game, administered the pats and for the next 50 minutes belted every Rough Rider who came his way.

Back in his hotel room, Lear was too tense to sit down and relax. He walked and talked while happy Calgary fans gathered on the streets below the hotel. It was one of the biggest moments of Lear's career and he tried, without much success, to talk tough about it. He wondered out loud whether the hollering fans outside would love him and his Stamps "when we lose a few games next year." They sure did love those Stampeders.

CHAPTER XV

THE TARPAULIN FIGHT

Nov. 26, 1949, at Toronto
Montreal Alouettes 28, Calgary Stampeders 15

This is the year of the fluffy little handkerchief and a huge piece of canvas known as a tarpaulin. In order, they evoked outlandish twitterings from amused football fans and howls of outrageous indignation from club officials.

The Canadian Rugby Union had decided that the horn, tooted by game officials since 1934 to denote a rules infraction, but not a stoppage of play, would have to go. The CRU ruled that a simpler way to get the message across to the players was to drop a handkerchief, marking the spot where the infraction took place.

This little ploy soon became known as "drop-the-hanky" and sportspage cartoonists fell all over themselves in the stampede to their drawing boards. They came up with some dandies, depicting fully-grown men in striped shirts daintily dropping scented, lace-embroidered hankies on the field.

The question of the tarpaulin was a serious matter. The 1949 Cup game was played on the Varsity Stadium field, a patchwork of snow and mud. Calgary club officials readily admitted the Stampeders had been beaten by a better club, but they fumed at CRU officials because they had not bought a tarpaulin to protect the field. "We've just witnessed some bare-faced larceny," said Tom Brooks, Calgary Stampeder president, after the game. "Fans don't want to see a bunch of guys sliding around on their bellies or their backsides in a national final. The fans were robbed."

Brooks, backed by his executive, said the Calgary club would buy a tarp for the CRU "if it was too damned stingy, bull-headed and near-sighted to buy one itself." His outburst was made at a party in the Toronto Men's Press Club quarters in downtown Toronto and the Calgary executive and club officials of other Western Conference teams hammered away at the CRU for another two years, until the Union paid $12,000 in 1951 for a field covering.

This year, in 1949, the Stampeders were back again with Les Lear working on a five-year contract as coach of the club. In the East, Lew Hayman had whipped up a powerhouse in Montreal. The Als had ended in a first-place Big Four tie with Toronto Argonauts in their founding year in 1946 (when they were known as the Hornets), placed third in 1947, second in 1948 and again this year.

The Als beat Ottawa 36-20 in the two-game total-point Eastern final. The Stamps finished on top in the West and squeaked past Saskatchewan Roughriders 22-21 in the total-point Western final. The Als quarterback was Frankie Filchock, who had a score to settle in the Grey Cup game. In 1945, Filchock, then with Washington Redskins, practically forward-passed Cleveland Rams out of the park but lost 15-14. Les Lear was a star on the Cleveland line that year.

Filchock's ball handling and passing sent Montreal into a 17-7 halftime lead and from there in the Stamps never did have much of a chance.

Backing up Filchock was Ches McCance, an old buddy of Lear's in their Winnipeg days in the 1930s. They had played together on the 1939 and 1941 Blue Bomber Cup-winning teams and their off-field activities were, at times, somewhat alarming. Jim Coleman, one of the best-known sports columnists in the country and a long-time friend of Lear, recalls the early 1930s when Lear and McCance were members of rival neighborhood gangs in Winnipeg. Let Coleman tell it:

"In the autumn of 1933 the Alexander Gang (of which Lear was a member) and the Dufferin Gang (of which McCance was a member) signed a bloody truce and the survivors joined Fred Ritter's Deer Lodge junior team. Ritter tried to beat some sense into their heads and, by the fall of 1936, they were ready to join the senior Blue Bombers. Ritter was ready for a strait jacket.

"The young gentlemen distinguished themselves on their first road trip to Calgary. Coach Bob Fritz was a tolerant man but he found it necessary to suspend Lear, McCance, Harry Badger and Bill Nairn who broke training rules so flagrantly that the startled Calgarians thought they had been invaded by hostile Indians . . . .

"They took to travelling in their bare feet and once there was really serious trouble in the dining car of a Canadian Pacific train when one of the wackier Bombers insisted upon testing a woman passenger's coffee with his bare toe before agreeing the java was cool enough for her palate . . . ."

Lear was a changed man when he took over the Stamps in 1948. He demanded discipline and hard work and he received it. Sixteen of Calgary's 1948 squad were not with the team this year. The missing included Fritzie Hanson, centre Chuck Anderson who had gone to the Als, and five players who left Calgary to attend McGill University in Montreal.

This was to be Lear's last Cup team. On Dec. 30, 1952, the Stampeder executive said thanks, but your contract is up and we are not renewing it. Lear went back to the thoroughbreds. A one-time groom and hot-walker, he gradually built up a stable as owner-trainer and campaigned around Ontario, Florida and California tracks. He did not particularly miss football. "Now," he said a few years later, "I don't have to roam the streets at night looking for football players who break the curfew. When you lock the barn at night, you know the horses will still be there in the morning."

Unfortunately, in all the 1949 post-game fuss about the tarpaulin, a Cup milestone passed unnoticed. Lew Hayman made history by coaching his fifth Grey Cup winner, a statistic that was to remain in the books. In 1969 Frank Clair of Ottawa Rough Riders matched it. And Canadian football was entering an era when the coach became the most expendable person on a club. If you coached a Cup winner— well, that is what you were hired to do. And who needs a loser?

And in 1949 Edmonton Eskimos returned to the Western Conference after a 10-year absence. Football's popularity was high, there was room on the gravy train and Eskimos climbed aboard.

CHAPTER XVI

THE GREAT MUD BOWL

Nov. 25, 1950, at Toronto
Toronto Argonauts 13, Winnipeg Blue Bombers 0

The under-statement of the decade was made this year in one six-word sentence by an abashed Canadian Rugby Union official: "We didn't think it would snow." Football fans and club officials shortened that sentence to read: "The CRU didn't think."

Scott Young, sports columnist with the Toronto Globe and Mail and later sports editor-columnist of the Toronto Telegram, wrote: "Every time I heard a car backfire Saturday night . . . I thought someone had shot a CRU official." A year before, CRU officials had been blistered by Western club officials because of far-from-ideal field conditions during the Grey Cup game. The CRU could have bought a tarpaulin for about $6,000. Colleges in the U.S. northwest, where weather conditions could be just as rough as in Toronto in late November, all had purchased tarpaulins, according to a survey conducted by the author.

The CRU decided to take its chances. Result: Eight inches of snow fell on the unprotected field the night before the Grey Cup game, followed by intermittent rain. At 10 o'clock the morning of the game, the field looked as if it had been the site of a plowing match.

A huge tractor truck hauled a mud-mired snow-removal truck off the field, leaving behind, of course, deep ruts. Crews of workmen descended on the field in hip-length rubber boots for frantic, last-minute repairs. This became the year of the Mud Bowl.

The life-saving occurred in full view of the 27,101 unbelieving spectators, but few realized what exactly was happening because the sight of men sliding up and down the crevices and through the goo and slop was commonplace.

The late Hec Crighton of Toronto, the judge of play, was the hero. Early in the game he spied large Buddy Tinsley of the Bombers lying face down in a puddle of water. He managed to get the 268-pounder facing skywards before, as they say on the beaches, he went under for the third time. In later years, Buddy guffawed about it. It simply wasn't so, he said. He was in full command of his senses and he was by no means drowning.

Argonauts and Blue Bombers were pass-happy clubs. Al Dekdebrun, an American, had taken over from all-Canadian Joe Krol as quarterback of Argos. His counterpart with the Western champions was Indian Jack Jacobs.

It was obvious that because of the condition of the field the pass was out and that the teams would have to adapt to the conditions. Argonauts did. Winnipeg didn't. Indian Jack had come to Canada this year via Green Bay Packers and Washington Redskins and had pitched Bombers to a 10-4 won-lost record in the West and a trip to Toronto in the three-game playoff against Edmonton Eskimos.

It soon became apparent that Jacobs and mud were incompatible. He had a horrible day and eventually was yanked in the fourth quarter for Pete Petrow, a young Canadian. Jacobs had fumbled twice in the second quarter in Winnipeg territory and each time Argonauts scored. Nick Volpe kicked 21- and 23-yard field goals. Jake Dunlap blocked a Jacobs' punt in the third quarter and in six plays Argos had the game's only touchdown, a one-yard plunge by Dekdebrun.

Later in the third quarter Dekdebrun intercepted a Jacobs pass and Krol kicked a single, his second of the day.

This was the first Cup victory for new Argo coach Frank Clair, a native of Hamilton, Ohio, who had played wing with Ohio State University, Washington Redskins, U.S. Army All-Stars and in 1948 and 1949, coached the University of Buffalo.

He brought in some new players—Ed (Buckets) Hirsch from Buffalo Bills, Ulysses (Crazy Legs) Curtis from Florida A&M, Billy Bass from Chicago Hornets, and John Kerns from Buffalo Bills, but most of his players were holdovers from the Teddy Morris-coached Argo clubs. These included Les Ascott, Jake Dunlap, Byron Karrys, Krol, Don Scott, Doug Smylie, Rod Smylie, Arnie Stocks, Ted Toogood, Nick Volpe and a few others.

Morris was a spectator at the 1950 Grey Cup game. "I never pulled any harder for Argos to win as I did this afternoon," he told reporters after the game.

This year became the start of a perilous time for coaches, particularly from the West. Frank (Butch) Larson, Bomber coach, had gone to

Toronto a week before Cup final to scout the Argonaut-Toronto Balmy Beach Eastern Canada playoff. High up on the Varsity Stadium roof press box he confided to a reporter that, win or lose, he would be out of a job after the Cup final. He was fired shortly after Bombers' return to Winnipeg. There were more firings to come.

CHAPTER XVII

THE GLENN DOBBS STORY

Nov. 24, 1951, at Toronto
Ottawa Rough Riders 21, Saskatchewan Roughriders 14

A place called Dobberville didn't show on a map of Canada or on any road map. The Canadian Almanac didn't list it. You couldn't find it in the Archives at Ottawa. Yet the name appeared on car licence plates, and on kids' sweat shirts and jeans.

But the Post Office department found out about it and letters or parcels addressed to "Dobberville, Canada" were automatically channelled to Regina.

The reason was a six-foot-three-inch friendly, triple-threat legend named Glenn Dobbs, who descended on Regina after a stint with the Los Angeles Dons and the old Brooklyn Dodgers. This 30-year-old Tulsa University grad had a personality and an Oklahoma drawl to match his numerous football talents.

The big blond quarterback so thoroughly dazzled the football populace that, before you could spell Saskatchewan, the city of Regina gleefully adopted the name Dobberville.

Dobbs arrived in June and, in this era when football and the Grey Cup were year-round topics across the country, the wheat province fans got down to serious talk of Dobbs bringing Saskatchewan its first Cup victory.

This, of course, was before he unveiled his throwing arm and his well-publicized right foot that could send a football 60 yards and more. Club executives thought so much of Dobbs that they gave him a two-year contract for $25,000, a figure far above the average in that period.

The Roughriders had been waiting since 1934 to get into the East-West final. They had an unimpressive no-win-seven-loss record in the national clashes and, suddenly, Saskatchewan was certain that Dobbs was the man to lead them out of the wilderness.

97

Fans for years told stories about their hero. For instance: when the club asked for volunteers to paint the fence surrounding Taylor Field, Dobbs was there with a pail of green paint.

When kids refused to drink their milk or eat their porridge, parents didn't worry. They knew that the threat of a phone call to Dobbs would get the kids back on the right track.

Dobbs could play football and he had the credentials to back him up. In the 1942 Sun Bowl game he helped Tulsa beat Texas Tech and then he played for the College All-Stars who beat the professional Washington Redskins 27-7 in the annual all-star game at Chicago.

In 1943 he was voted the outstanding player of the All-Star game, turned pro in 1946 with the Brooklyn Dodgers of the All-American Conference, and went to the Los Angeles Dons in 1947.

With this background, Roughriders could not be blamed for believing that this big smiling American would at least get them into the Western playoffs and, who knows, right into the Cup final.

Dobbs had turned down offers—and more money—from Chicago Bears to play for Regina and fans soon sensed that at least the club would be definite Cup contenders. Roughriders started the season by winning three straight, including a 30-1 victory over Winnipeg Blue Bombers, the 1950 Western champs. Roughriders won the Western title, beating Edmonton Eskimos 19-18 in the final. Then, it was on to Toronto and a date with Ottawa.

Bookmakers, who for years had quoted the Eastern champions at odds ranging from 3 to 1 to 5 to 1, weren't so sure this time. The final line was Ottawa 6 to 5, although Roughriders let everyone know that Jack Russell, their fine pass receiver, would be out of the game with a torn knee cartillage.

One thing fans didn't know was that Dobbs himself was an unlikely starter. Forty-eight hours before the kickoff, the Roughies held a secret workout at a field near the waterfront. Out of this came sad news. Dobbs had three broken ribs and sprained knee ligaments.

That wasn't the end of it. The night before the game the Canadian Rugby Union announced that Bob Sandberg, their big bulldozing back, was not eligible to play.

The Roughriders wanted to play him as a Canadian, but the CRU said this wasn't possible. Sandberg had played in Canada for three years starting in 1947 and was line coach of Winnipeg in 1950 but the CRU stuck to its original decision made in August of that year that classed him as an import.

The ruling this time was that he had not completed four continuous years of playing in Canada. That, according to the rules of the CRU, was a requirement for Canadian status. The ruling reminded Saskatchewan fans of 1936 when the Roughriders won the Western title and then were tossed out of Cup contention because the club had not gone along with the CRU's ruling on imports. That year the CRU had ruled that only Americans resident in Canada before Jan. 1 were eligible to play.

Roughriders therefore had five ineligible players on its roster in 1936 and they volunteered to drop these for the big game but the CRU remained firm in its decision. And here, in 1951, the Roughriders were again blunted by CRU regulations, but this time they accepted the ruling without a great deal of fuss.

Grey Cup day dawned clea and crisp. The CRU had bought a $12,000 tarpaulin and it was laid down over Varsity Stadium a couple of days before the game, but it really wasn't needed. The field was in perfect shape. A crowd of 27,341, the largest to watch a football game in Canada to date, was at Varsity. And it appeared that just possibly an upset was in the works.

Dobbs put the Roughriders ahead 2-0 with a pair of towering singles. Ottawa, missing only defensive half Ted McClarty who was injured in a wild, fist- and elbow-swinging Eastern Canada final game against Sarnia Imperials, the ORFU champions, soon took command. They built up a 20-2 lead in the final quarter when Saskatchewan capitalized on a pair of Ottawa fumbles to score two touchdowns. By then it was too little, too late.

Dobbs, who wore a plastic girdle from his waist to his armpits to protect his three broken ribs and whose knee had been shot with novacaine, completed six of 18 passes, including a touchdown strike to Jack Nix in the final drive.

Sully Glasser scored Saskatchewan's other touchdown on a 10-yard plunge and Red Ettinger kicked the converts. Benny MacDonnell, Alton Baldwin and Pete Karpuk scored Ottawa touchdowns. Bob Gain kicked the converts, and singles were added by Bruce Cummings and quarter Tom O'Malley.

Jake Dunlap, who later became a lawyer in Ottawa, was kicked out of the game in the final 20 minutes, the first player in Cup history to get the gate. His offence: roughing the kicker. Loyal Saskatchewan fans met the Roughriders on their return home with signs reading: "To the Roughriders, You're Still Our Champions." They still loved Dobbs and, as he was accustomed to saying, "my ol' gang."

There was one unhappy fellow in the crowd: Coach Harry (Black Jack) Smith. He was fired and he knew it before the big game, just as Butch Larson of the Winnipeg Cup finalists knew he was through before the 1950 final. But, shucks, everyone in Dobberville knew all along that their big, smiling hero, Glenn Dobbs, was the real coach and leader throughout the 1951 season.

CHAPTER XVIII

THE DECLINE OF KROL

Nov. 29, 1952, at Toronto
Toronto Argonauts 21, Edmonton Eskimos 11

No. 55 on the uniform was right. The dark blue/light blue club colors were correct. But the setting—well, it was just as if Gordie Howe had been shunted to a utility spot at the end of the bench and Mickey Mantle had been relegated to No. 9 from the cleanup spot in the batting order.

There, for everyone to see at Varsity Stadium was Joe (King) Krol picking up bench slivers. The 27,391 sellout crowd at the Bloor St. bowl where Krol had thrilled thousands of fans over the years didn't know it, but it was the end of the line for him.

This was Joe Krol's swan song to Grey Cup play and the man who played such a tremendous role in Argonauts' three straight Cup victories over Winnipeg Blue Bombers starting in 1945, did not receive enough playing time to work up a sweat. He trotted onto the field only on third-down-and-punt situations.

It was the finish of a big-time career for the great triple-threat player, the Cup's all-time scoring champion, one of the finest Canadian-born players of all time, an all-star in every league he played in going back to 1938, and twice winner of the Eastern Canada scoring title.

He was remembered as the passing, catching, running, place-kicking, punting wizard who semed to be a whole football team by himself in the late 1930s and in the 1940s. He was the man who brought Argonaut fans to their feet with last-minute, or even last-second, feats that turned almost certain defeat into victory.

Joe seemed to save his great days for the East-West finals, particularly in that 1945-47 period against the Bombers. He had what appeared to be a casual, loping, easy-flowing approach to the game and his accomplishments made his name a household word.

The sparkle went out of his star after the three consecutive Cup

101

victories over Winnipeg and with the frantic rush for imports. Clubs wanted the Joe Blows from the U.S. instead of the Joe Krols from Canada. But few players in the long history of the Cup final have been as dominating as Krol.

This year, 1952, was his seventh Grey Cup appearance and the sixth time he had been with a winner. Ironically, it was the first time he failed to hit the scoreboard since his Cup debut in 1943 when he contributed seven points as Hamilton Flying Wildcats defeated Winnipeg RCAF-Bombers 23-14.

He had added another 23 points, mainly in spectacular fashion, for a Cup-total of 30, a mark that has stood throughout the years although the touchdown value had been increased to six points from the traditional five. None of the big names, the glamor ball-carrying and pass-catching imports, could match his record. He had a play for every situation: the swift kick, the onside kick. He could throw a pass with uncanny accuracy, catch a pass, play defence, drop-kick and he seemed to produce his best punts with a wet ball, against the wind, or when rushed by a bad snap or given poor protection by the men up front.

He had a knack of turning what would be considered impossible situations completely around. He was a super-star and, at times, fans treated him like a bum. They didn't realize that he was going all out because his easy-flowing style appeared to be so effortless. He had the natural ability and there was little he couldn't do on a football field.

This year, though, Joe was another number on the Argonaut club coached by Frank Clair. His quarterback was Nobby Wirkowski, 23-year-old University of Miami in Ohio graduate who had taken over in mid-season 1951 when Al Dekdebrun was cut. It was Clair's second Cup victory and the last for Argonauts as the club entered the 1970 season.

The Eskimos of 1952, coached by Frank Filchock, had beaten Winnipeg in a wild Western final and travelled to Toronto with hundreds of fans sporting "I Like Esks" buttons. There were not many others who liked the Westerners, particularly the bookmakers who installed Argonauts 9-to-5 favorites.

Eskimos, rebuilt from scratch in 1949 by Annis Stukus who was let go after the 1951 season, moved into a first quarter lead on the first of two touchdowns by Normie Kwong. Argos moved ahead 15-5 in the second on touchdowns by Wirkowski and Billy Bass, a pair of converts and a field goal by Red Ettinger. Kwong got his second touchdown in the third quarter, converted by Wilbur Snyder, and Argos wrapped up their 10th Cup victory late in the game when Zeke O'Connor, in the clear, took a Wirkowski pass and scored the clinching touchdown.

This was Edmonton's third apearance in the Cup since the East-West final was born in 1921, but they were to be heard from in a couple of years when a few players named Jackie Parker, Bernie Faloney, and Johnny Bright joined Kwong in the backfield. That was when the West really socked it to the East.

Meanwhile, a surprising development occurred in the West. Glenn Dobbs took over as coach of Saskatchewan Roughriders and ended up with egg all over his face. The Roughriders finished last and, unbelievably, the fans still loved their handsome hero. The Riders won only one of eight home games, a statistic that in ordinary times would make any hard-bitten fan take a wide detour of Taylor Field in Regina. But not those football-loving fans. They filled the park every game. In one contest, the Dobber dropped two easy passes and the crowd gave him a terrific ovation. The front office apparently didn't share this esteem. "I'm anxious to return, no matter what kind of a job they offer me," Dobbs said at the tailend of the season. He was around in 1953, but Frankie Filchock had taken over the Roughrider coaching chores and Dobbs confined himself to field activities.

The shine was beginning to come off Dobberville. And it had vanished completely from Joe King Krol.

CHAPTER XIX

ON FIRING COACHES

Nov. 28, 1953, at Toronto
Hamilton Tiger-Cats 12, Winnipeg Blue Bombers 6

The situation was normal in the West this year. Winnipeg Blue Bombers' coach George Trafton was fired. In this explosive, anything-goes era of Canadian professional football, a coach was an expendable commodity. The woods were full of men who made an occupation of pacing up and down the sidelines in front of a bench full of husky footballers.

The logic of club executives in the West, at least to outsiders, was strange, bewildering and stubbornly consistent. But the thinking of the front office people was clear to the coaches: Make it to the Grey Cup final and you're fired. It wasn't as cold-blooded as this but club officials had established a pattern and they undoubtedly had good reason to make their policy stick, but it did seem odd that success should be punishable by banishment.

Consider this: starting in 1950, every Western coach who brought his club to the national classic knew before he made the trip to Toronto that he was due for the chop. Here's the list: 1950: Frank (Butch) Larson, Winnipeg. Bombers lost 13-0 to Toronto Argonauts. 1951: Harry (Black Jack) Smith, Saskatchewan Roughriders. The Riders lost 21-14 to Ottawa Rough Riders. 1952: Frank Filchock, Edmonton Eskimos. The Eskimos lost 21-11 to Argonauts. And in 1953: Trafton.

There were other casualties in the coaching ranks. Les Lear, who took Calgary Stampeders to the Cup final in 1948 and won 12-7 over Ottawa Rough Riders, and who was there in 1949 when the Stamps lost 28-15 to Montreal Alouettes, was bounced at the end of the 1952 season.

So was Glenn Dobbs of Saskatchewan Roughriders. The thinking here was starightforward enough because the Roughies were a resounding flop in 1952 with a last-place finish in the Western Conference.

These developments, of course, were only byplays to the Trafton firing. It was widely known that the former Chicago Bear, who still had a year to go on a three-year contract, was headed for the coaches' graveyard. Even if Bombers won the Cup. He was an outspoken, no-nonsense, tough-tongued man and anyone who got in his way was unceremoniously dealt with: club executives, sports writers, radio broadcasters, or his own players. He had a job to do and, logically enough, there was no way he would stand for interference from anybody.

The situation came to a head in the third game of the best-of-three Western final against Edmonton Eskimos. It was late in the third quarter, Bombers were behind 18-6 and into the game went Indian Jack Jacobs. It was widely reported—and vigorously denied at the time by the parties involved—that frantic club officials had ordered Trafton to insert his all-star quarterback into the contest in place of Joe Zaleski.

Whoever made the decision had great powers of perception. Big Jake threw 20 passes in 25 minutes. He completed 14 for 243 yards and three touchdowns and Bombers won the right to a Grey Cup berth with a 30-24 decision on a last-minute pass interception that went for a touchdown. The victory sealed Winnipeg's trip to Toronto, and Trafton's exit.

Bombers went through the motions to beat Toronto Balmy Beach of the Ontario Rugby Football Union 24-4 in the first sudden-death final in Western Canada involving an Eastern team. Then, it was a head-on collision against Tiger-Cats with more than 2,000 Winnipeg fans in the stands at Varsity Stadium. It was Bombers' second trip in four years, since the famous 1950 Mud Bowl at Varsity when field conditions were such that any sort of an aerial offensive was out. Winnipeg did try 15 that year, completed three for only 48 yards.

But that was in the past. This time the field was in great shape, the sky was clear and the temperature was 38 degrees. Jake's throwing arm was well greased for this one and the 27,313 crowd witnessed a thriller. Jacobs' passing arm demolished Grey Cup records as he got his shots away on the gallop while running for his life against such Ticat brutes as Vince Scott, Jake Gaudaur, Vince Mazza, Ed Bevan and company.

Jake tried 46 passes, 12 more than the previous high of 34 by Claude Arnold of Edmonton in 1952. He completed 28, far ahead of the old Cup mark of 19 set in 1949 by Keith Spaith of Calgary and his total passing yardage was 326 to Arnold's 261 in 1952. Most of these statistics were to be erased from the book in later years, but his performance was a standout.

With all this, there was one glaring gap in the statistics: Indian Jack did not throw one touchdown pass. But be came close as time ran out. It was a hunch, a gamble or whatever by Ticats' Lou Kusserow that robbed Bombers of a TD pass that, with the convert, would have sent the Cup into overtime.

Jacobs had moved Bombers from their own seven-yard line to the Tiger-Cats four in 11 plays, including six passes. There was time left for one play. Big Jake reared back, spied Tom Casey all alone at the one-yard line, and let fly. At the same time Kusserow, who was covering ing Neill Armstrong in the end zone, peeled off, made a dash for Casey, and the ball and the Columbia University star arrived at the same time.

The ball squirted out of Casey's arms as he was hit—the only pass in five he had missed during the game—and the scoreboard clock moved to its final stop. The crowd gave Jacobs a standing ovation, and lost in all the excitment was the dazzling play of a Ticat.

Quarterback Ed (Butch) Songin was his name. He was a tremendous performer and few people realized that he was the fifth quarterback used this season by Coach Carl Voyles in an effort to mould a winning combination. He expertly mixed ground plays with an aerial game that sent his receivers scooting 137 yards on 10 completions in 22 attempts. Songin also scored a Hamilton touchdown in the opening quarter on a one-yard plunge and put Tiger-Cats ahead 12-6 in the third when he caught Vito Ragazzo with a 15-yard pass at the Winnipeg 40 and he went the rest of the way for a 55-yard pass-and-run touchdown. Tip Logan kicked the converts.

Winnipeg's lone touchdown was scored by Eddie James on a one-yard third-quarter plunge. Bud Korchak kicked the convert and it was a 6-6 game until Songin and Ragazzo got together for their winning five-pointer. Also in this game was Jake Gaudaur, son of a famous father whose sculling exploits made him one of the all-time-great Canadian athletes. Jake Jr. had retired from football, but he was talked into playing one more year—in 1953—at his familiar snap position.

After this game, Bombers and Tiger-Cats left the Cup scene for three years while Jackie Parker and his Edmonton Eskimo friends and Sam Etcheverry and company from Montreal Alouettes occupied centre stage.

106

A couple of off-beat incidents during Cup day livened up the proceedings in 1953. Neither involved a player. One concerned a hearse, Harry McBrien of Toronto, the Grey Cup co-ordinator, and Billy Wray of Montreal, a football official and an undertaker. Harry had some last-minute chores to clean up and was detained in his Royal York hotel room until shortly before the kickoff. Wray was with him.

With time getting short, the two dashed out of the hotel and couldn't find a taxicab to take them to the stadium. Wray phoned an undertaker friend. Their transportation arrived shortly after and the pair were delivered to Varsity—in a hearse. With hundreds of persons looking on, they jauntily stepped out and walked into the stadium. After the game, Harry was presented with the wooden box that had held the Cup. Lugging the empty box and with Wray at his side, Harry couldn't find a taxi. Wray spotted a motorcycle policeman, walked over to him and pointed to McBrien as he talked. The policeman nodded, roared away and in a couple of minutes returned with a cab and two other motorcycle officers.

They provided an escort to McBrien's hotel, left their bikes and saw McBrien and Wray to their suite.

When the officers had left, McBrien asked Wray what he had done to command such attention. "I told the officer the Grey Cup receipts were in the box." Meanwhile, in the same hotel, Len Back, the bowler-hatted manager of Hamilton senior clubs since 1928, was swapping stories with other fans in the Blue Bomber suite. Someone from the Bomber club mentioned he would love to see the Grey Cup.

Always-obliging Len hustled to his room, a couple of floors down, wrapped up the trophy and stepped into an elevator. "What's in the package?" asked a drunken fellow passenger. "The Grey Cup," replied Len. "Smart guy, eh?" said the stranger who promptly planted a fist in Len's face. Len suffered a black eye, a cut face and his glasses were broken. But he made it back to the party, with the Cup.

CHAPTER XX

JACKIE PARKER
BECOMES A LEGEND

Nov. 27, 1954, at Toronto
Edmonton Eskimos 26, Montreal Alouettes 25

In 1954 Vancouver had its hands full with the British Empire Games, and with Annis Stukus. Frantic last-minute preparations were being made for the Games which brought together an exciting collection of world-ranking athletes from the Commonwealth countries. This was no minor undertaking and Vancouver citizens pitched in to make these the greatest since the Games were first held in Hamilton in 1930.

Keeping right in step was Stuke, the talkative Lithuanian who was hired to sell pro football in British Columbia. Stuke, who had a similar job when Edmonton Eskimos rejoined the Western Conference in 1949 and made a success of it until he was let out in 1951, had a two-fold job. First, he had to get the bodies to fill the roster of the newly-born British Columbia Lions and, second, to sell the game to the natives. Stuke was right in his element in this era, when pro football was a year-round topic of conversation. But he had plenty of opposition from a horde of Vancouver people who were promoting the Games.

To help Stuke there was news from other football clubs. Edmonton Eskimos signed Bernie Faloney, a 21-year-old quarterback from the University of Maryland who had been everybody's all-everything in 1953 in the U.S. They also signed Jackie Parker, 22-year-old halfback/-quarterback from Mississippi State whose drawl was as long as his gimpy legs.

BE Games officials wouldn't be out-done. They became name-droppers. They had Roger Bannister of England, the man who made world headlines by becoming the first person to crack the four-minute-mile barrier. They also had John Landy of Australia, who had beaten Bannister's mark and, at the time, was the fastest miler in the world.

The Eskimos had signed Pop Ivy, the split-T expert from Oklahoma who succeeded Darryl Royal, another Oklahoma grad who introduced this ball-control system in 1953 and almost made it to the Grey Cup. Ivy made one big change—the double-fullback offence and he had a couple of bodies to make it click—Johnny Bright and Normie Kwong. Talk of football died as the Games got down to the wire with the influx of hundreds of athletes from all parts of the Commonwealth. The Games themselves produced some fantastic performances, climaxed during the blazing-hot final day when Bannister and Landy ran what has been forever tagged as the "Miracle Mile." Each ran the distance in under four minutes, the first time two men had accomplished the feat in a race and piling thrill on thrill was the unforgettable second when Landy, in front by a couple of strides, peeked over his left shoulder as Bannister thundered past him on the right and on to victory.

The 25,000 fans at Empire Stadium knew that they were watching track history and their elation and enthusiasm was abrupty squelched by the agonizing sight of England's Jim Peters. He wobbled into the stadium for the final couple of hundred yards of the 26-mile 385-yard marathon. Time and again he stumbled, sprawled to the track, got up and dragged a paralyzed left leg in an unsuccessful bid to cross the finish line.

Nothing in sports this year could match the Bannister-Landy spectacle and the horrifying moments of Peters' agony. That is what sports observers said but on Saturday, Nov. 27, at Varsity Stadium in Toronto, millions of television viewers and a screaming, unbelieving mob of 27,321 watched a gangling, shuffle-footed boy from Ole Mississipp' gallop 85 yards for a touchdown that blew the lid off one of the greatest Cup celebrations in history.

This was the day that Jackie Parker became a legend in Canadian football. His 15-second run down the sidelines with Johnny Bright striding right along beside him, came just 3½ minutes from time and, with the pressure-cooker convert kicked by Bob Dean, gave Eskimos their 26-25 victory over the Als.

It went into the books as a stunning, bewildering upset for the Als, one of the most shocking reversals—to Easterners only—since Winnipegs went unheralded into Hamilton in 1935 and defeated the Tigers 18-12. Ranked alongside it was that slightly-overcast, 44-degree Saturday afternoon in 1948 in the same stadium when Les Lear patted his kids "on the buttocks" early in the contest, placed his bulk on the line and his Calgary Stampeders upset Ottawa Rough Riders 12-7.

Parker's grab-and-run crusher came at a time when the Als were ahead 25-20 and on the march to a clinching touchdown. It all popped so fast that spectators and TV viewers alike weren't sure what happened. Simply, it was a blind, weird attempted lateral of sorts to nowhere by the Als' Chuck Hunsinger.

"He had a brain storm," said Als Coach Doug (Peahead) Walker. "He just threw the ball away." Edmonton fans couldn't have cared less about Hunsinger's brainstorm or whatever. All they knew and cared about was the story the scoreboard had to tell. Unbelieving Eastern fans had statistics to prove that between the goal lines the Als gave Eskimos a good whomping—37 to 25 in first downs, 698 yards passing and rushing against 567, 23 of 33 pass completions against 10 of 23.

But they had to face a fact of football life. The only statistics that win ball games are the points kept by the scorekeeper. Hunsinger didn't wait long for the post-mortems and what the hindsight boys had to say. He gathered up his wife at a downtown hotel and headed back to the U.S. He came back to Canada the following year, suffered a leg injury and that was the end of a fine football career that had to be clouded in one play.

The Eskimos, of course, went into the game as under-dogs. Easterners hadn't been exposed to the crushing ground attack of the Eskimos and even if they had it wouldn't have meant a thing because they figured the quick-striking passing game was the only way to win football games.

Etcheverry had proved that in the East. And, when it came time to play for the Cup, Eastern followers could see only Etcheverry throwing strikes to Red O'Quinn and company. They could see only Alex Webster, the club's big find this year, and a couple of other backfielders ripping through the Edmonton front wall. Just to keep things honest and set the Als up for the pass.

Odds ranged from 3-to-1 to 5-to-1 and it was money in the bank for the guys who gave the odds—that is, until Parker practically genuflected to pick up that loose ball and take off. In the final analysis, Edmonton's victory was fashioned on a combination of circumstances: Bernie Faloney's magic ball-handling, his abacadabra of here it is, there it ain't; Parker's touchdown, the always-alert Edmonton line and the final convert of sure-footed Bob Dean who hadn't missed the extra point all season. He realized it would have been a terrible time to miss with the score all knotted up.

110

Then, there was Eagle Keys. He had suffered a hairline fracture to the main bone in his left leg just before the end of the first quarter. After that, he hobbled back onto the field to snap the ball for all of Edmonton's punts, Dean's third-quarter field goal. But he couldn't get off the bench after Parker's touchdown and centre linebacker Bill Briggs snapped the ball for the game-winning convert.

Keys' leg fracture was discovered only when he went to hospital after the game and x-rays showed a "hairline crack." Etcheverry got his name in the record books, and so did Red O'Quinn, but they never did get around to drinking champagne out of the Cup while with the Als.

Sam threw three touchdown passes, a Cup record for one game that finally was eclipsed by Ottawa's Russ Jackson in 1969. Red, who later became general manager of Ottawa and then with Montreal in 1970, had four entries—a 93-yard touchdown run, longest in Cup history; two touchdown passes caught, later equalled, in one game; 13 passes caught and 316 yards gained on passes.

And Stuke? He had a bunch of players who, he promised, would make the Lions Roar in '54. Every football expert in the land predicted the Lions would finish fifth in the five-team Western Conference. They did, but that was no disgrace. No pro club could expect to come up with a winning hand on the first deal. Stuke said the Lions would Come Alive In '55. They didn't, and fidgety club executives let Stukus go after the 1955 season.

People were running out of slogans. There were other troublesome moments in football in 1954.

Ontario Rugby Football Union officials had long ago sniffed a power play by the Big Four and Western Conferences to toss the ORFU out of the Cup playoffs. Relations were strained and, at times, bitter.

Observers felt the ORFU had hurried things along a week before the Cup final when Kitchener-Waterloo Dutchmen, ORFU champions and farm club of the Eskimos, met the Esks at Edmonton in the Cup semi-final. Eskimos won 38-6 but the game developed into a tong war and it was a cinch that the big boys were more than ever determined to toss the ORFU out on its ear. The risk of player injuries was too great.

There was another war front, this time in the U.S. and Canadian pro football—specifically, the Eastern Big Four—hit gold. The National Collegiate Athletic Association in the U.S. took its "Game Of The

Week away from NBC in April and awarded it to ABC. Another TV outfit, Dumont, held all rights to National League games and NBC found itself without a Saturday afternoon football telecast.

It made a deal to televise Big Four games over its U.S. coast-to-coast network and included the Cup final in the package deal. The experiment was not a crashing success, but it did give Americans an insight into the Canadian game and in this era more and more American college and NFL players were happy to get a piece of the action—plus bundles of cash—in Canada.

It became apparent that all hell would break loose between the NFL and Canadian clubs unless something was done to stop the Canadian raiding. It came much sooner than anyone expected.

CHAPTER XXI

THE SONSHINE CAPER

Nov. 26, 1955, at Vancouver
Edmonton Eskimos 34, Montreal Alouettes 19

Undeclared football war was busting out everywhere. It was waged in an uptown Toronto apartment, in every big league football city in the East and West, in the United States and in cities housing one of the bulwarks of the game in Canada—the Ontario Rugby Football Union.

No shots were fired but Harry Sonshine, a one-time player with Queen's University in Kingston, Ont., and Toronto Argonauts, was called a warmonger. Argos, out of the Big Four playoff picture in 1953 and 1954, shot the works in a no-limit talent raiding of National Football League clubs in the U.S. Sonshine was the instigator, the man with what seemed to be unlimited cash at his disposal.

The NFL screamed foul. NFL clubs vowed they would run "those Canadians out of business." Sonshine was called a "terrible black eye to Canadian football" by executives of other Canadian clubs. There were court cases over player rights, threats and predictions of doom— and Sonshine went his merry way. Nothing would stop him, and Argonauts, from building a contender. And the irony of it all was that he never did get the club to the Grey Cup before he departed the scene after about 18 headline-creating months of trying.

The Big Four executive threatened to shoot Argos down. It did not mean a thing. Big, gruff, Bill Ross, president of Argonauts, told them to go right ahead. He, and everyone else in football, knew that the Big Four couldn't survive without the Toronto club and that a Big Three of Montreal, Ottawa and Hamilton would be a farce.

The Big Four finally restored some sort of harmony within its ranks, got together with the Western Conference for a meeting in Vancouver and awarded the 1955 Grey Cup final to the West Coast city. It was the first time the East-West classic would be played west of the Ontario-Manitoba border. This precedent-shattering meeting also set at 10 the

113

number of U.S. imports each team could dress for the Cup final, set Oct. 15 as the cutoff date for registration of players and set a top price of $7.50 for Cup tickets.

The big leagues had passed legislation giving them voting control of the Canadian Rugby Union. And one of the first pieces of business was to tell the ORFU that it did not want the Union cluttering up the Grey Cup picture.

The once-proud ORFU, now reduced to farm-club status of Big Four and WIFU teams, knew it was licked, although some niceties were observed. The Big Four and WIFU didn't exactly boot out the ORFU— it simply arranged schedules which would not allow time for a challenge from the Union. ORFU officials, well aware of the move for months, took it as back-alley talk and they were prepared to fight a battle they knew they couldn't win. Previously, they had taken the fight into the open, behind closed doors—anywhere.

"We'll be back next year," thundered ORFU President Don Downey of Toronto. He, and other officials of his league, knew that this was just whistling, but they wanted everyone to know they would not yield without a good fight. A 46-year Cup tradition was broken and teams from the 73-year-old circuit faded out with this record: 14 Cup final appearances, seven wins, seven losses.

Meanwhile, Sonshine was crashing into trouble. In December, 1954, he blithely announced that none of the Argonaut imports would be back. He staged an open battle with Coach Frank Clair, vowed quarterback Nobby Wirkowski had to go. He travelled from New York to California, and more or less told NFL players to name their own price. What started out as a strictly local story in Toronto blossomed out in sports-page headlines across the country.

Sonshine called press conferences at his uptown apartment, which turned out to be another battleground of sorts. He produced off-the-record lists of NFL players he had ticketed for delivery to Argos and, before anyone really knew what was happening, Toronto football reporters started quarrelling among themselves, and with Sonshine, over press releases.

There were a series of broken confidences, and more fighting. He signed quarterback Tom Dublinski and tackle Gil Mains from Detroit Lions. He signed Billy Albright and Billy Shipp, a couple of over-sized linemen from New York Giants. All signed no-cut contracts. The Lions

114

took court action and lost. Clair quit. Wirkowski was fired. Coach Bill Swiacki from the Giants was hired.

When officials eventually got around to giving the game back to the players, Edmonton Eskimos and Montreal Alouettes proceeded to win the West and the East and get set for another Cup confrontation. The Als just made it as Sonshine's gamble almost paid off. Argos finished third behind the Larks and Hamilton Tiger-Cats in the Big Four, defeated Ticats 32-28 in the semi-final and lost 38-36 to the Als in the final. The Esks, with Jackie Parker now calling the shots at quarterback, were out to prove that the 26-25 triumph in 1954 was no fluke. The Als—well, they still had Sam Etcheverry, the biggest gambler on a Canadian football field.

Parker made Mississippi magic with his football hands and proved a paradoxical point: The shortest distance to any given goal line is along the ground. He did everything but stick the ball in his ear and there were times when fans, players and even an official didn't know where to look for the thing. They couldn't find it most of the afternoon. Hand-offs, reverses, off-tackle shots and end runs exploded from the ball-control Eskimo attack and the Als unabashedly admitted later that Parker's sleight-of-hand tricks and handoffs to fullbacks Johnny Bright and Normie Kwong—particularly Kwong—had them groping.

The crowd of 39,417—largest in Cup history who contributed to a gross gate of $197,182.91—could follow the ball only the few times Montreal had possession. Even a game official was perplexed. On one play, Kwong barrelled through the line, was brought down and the official standing right there was all set to blow his whistle until Kwong looked up, pointed to his quarterback who was racing around end with the ball. Kwong recalled the play. "The official looked at me, I looked at him and he ran away. That was all there was to it."

But it wasn't. Kwong carried 29 times for a net gain of 135 yards and the Als, just to be sure, went after him every time he hit the line. They were convinced each time that he had the ball tucked in his belly. Normie, who played on Calgary's 1948 Cup champions as an 18-year-old rookie and who was reported to have been paid $250 for that season, scored two touchdowns. So did Johnny Bright. Bob Heydenfeldt took a touchdown pass from Parker for the other TD and Bob Dean kicked the converts, a field goal and a single.

Pat Abbruzzi, who had taken over the spot left vacant by the departure of Alex Webster, scored Montreal's first touchdown and Etcheverry passed to Hal Patterson for the other two. Bud Korchak kicked the converts and was credited with a single in the final quarter when his field goal attempt was wide. Fans in the end zone pounced on the ball and officials—after a huddle—allowed the point.

The second victory of the West over the East in successive years set off a riot of carnival demonstrations that roared on for 12 hours. Hotels, restaurants and the downtown section of Vancouver couldn't begin to sort themselves out until long after thousands of wild-eyed visitors had headed eastward for home. The replay was well underway. The consensus was that the Als were lucky to be alive after this match and the only way to stop the crisp, finely-honed Eskimo ground attack would be to use bullets.

Montreal's aerial offensive, although formidable in the statistics, was ineffective. Eskimos allowed them the short passes and methodically blanketed the long ones. Cup records exploded all over Empire Stadium. Eskimos gained 448 yards on the ground, surpassing by 72 yards the previous mark of 376 set in 1932 by Hamilton Tigers. Etcheverry completed a record 30 passes for a record 508 yards.

And the game saw the fewest punts in a Cup final. Each club kicked six times, one less than the 1954 mark established when Edmonton punted 10 times and Montreal three. Everything was not roses for the Eskimos. Club auditors came up with a balance sheet showing a deficit of $10,807 on the year's operations. It was the club's first loss in seven years and it arose mainly from a revenue drop of $55,000. That is the price Eskimos had to pay as the finest club in the country.

They weren't the only losers. Scalpers lost a bundle. They were selling $2 standing room at the stadium for $1 an hour before the kickoff with possible takers scared away from the area by sellout reports downtown. Meanwhile, Jackie Parker and mates weren't through yet. They went home to brew up some more magic for 1956. Out of that came Don Getty, a young player who proved that, along with the Normie Kwongs and others, Canadians had a place in the country's greatest sports spectacle.

CHAPTER XXII

THE SIX POINT TOUCHDOWN

Nov. 24, 1956, at Toronto
Edmonton Eskimos 50, Montreal Alouettes 27

Damn Yankees, hollered the traditionalists. The diehards, who had suffered year by year as the Canadian Rugby Union took bites out of the U.S. rule book to provide a wide-open brand of football for the spectators, received a severe jolt on March 26 at Toronto.

On that date, the CRU increased the value of the touchdown to six points from five. It brought the value into line with the Americans, and that is what the shouting was all about. The thinking behind the move was solid. In this age of fieldgoal specialists, the rulemakers concluded that a converted touchdown should be worth more than two placements.

There certainly was a lot more to it than the CRU simply making the change. A month before, the Big Four and WIFU got together to form the Canadian Football Council and this was the outfit that did it—the CRU existed in name only. The Big Four and WIFU ran the show. They had met behind closed doors and decided on revaluation and everything was cut and dried—at least, on the surface—when they met in open session to rubber-stamp their decisions. The late Leo Dandurand of Montreal, Big Four spokesman, rattled a few bones when he got to his feet and spoke out against the six-point change.

The initial shock over with, delegates hurriedly held on-the-spot secret consultations and convinced Leo that, as Big Four spokesman, he was compelled to carry out the wishes of his associates. Leo consented.

In a couple of years everything was just fine with the traditionalists. Football men never did tinker with the distinctively Canadian single point, the five-yard leeway given to the punt-return men and the free-wheeling backfield-in-motion rules.

And this year the Big Four decided to bring some semblance of order into its house. It appointed a commissioner, 62-year-old Ottawa

Magistrate Allan J. Fraser. The West confirmed reappointment of its commissioner, G. Sydney Halter of Winnipeg.

Everything wasn't roses however. Ralph Cooper of Hamilton, chairman of the Canadian Football Council and representing the nine Canadian clubs, met NFL Commissioner Bert Bell of the NFL in Philadelphia to plot the general outline of an agreement to halt player raids. The date was Feb. 15 and two days later Baltimore Colts of the NFL announced they had signed Billy Vessels, a former Oklahoma star who played with Edmonton prior to entering the U.S. army. He was still Edmonton property. Nothing serious developed, but it was an indication of how clubs operated.

This sideline activity over with, it remained for an American coach, Pop Ivy of Edmonton Eskimos, to give a morale booster to every young Canadian football player with aspirations of becoming a big-league quarterback. Pop decided it wasn't necessary to go along with American quarterbacks to win the Grey Cup. He named Don Getty as his starting quarter against the Alouettes. Getty? Players in the senior intercollegiate union in the East knew him well. So did pro scouts who had compiled a good book on him and who rated this college grad as an excellent prospect.

One has to go back a year to get the picture. In 1955, the CRU set up for the first time a national draft of Canadian college players and Getty, who had graduated with honors in business administration from the University of Western Ontario at London, was a natural for the pro ranks. He had led Mustangs to three Eastern college titles in four years.

Eskimos, already loaded with quarterback talent such as the incomparable Jackie Parker, got him. The usual procedure was to bill these young college kids, particularly quarterbacks, as the find of the decade and then assign them to the end of the bench where they could at least be close to the action on the field. Getty was no exception. In 1955, he was understudy to Parker. It was the same story in 1956 until the second game of the best-of-three Western final against Winnipeg Blue Bombers.

Ivy sent him in and was impressed with his performance. He decided to take the gamble. The 22-year-old Getty would get the starting assignment in the Cup final. He moved Parker to a halfback position, inserted the 190-pound, six-foot-two youngster into the slot, and came up with instant success.

118

It was the first time a Canadian had started as quarterback in a Cup final since 1947 when 130-pound Fred Doty handled Toronto Argonauts who won a 10-9 thriller over the Bombers. Pop undoubtedly had a hunch. He figured the Als, defeated twice in as many years by the Eskimos because they didn't know how to straighten out Edmonton's split-T offence, would still be confused even with a rookie signal-caller.

He was right. Getty directed the attack throughout the 60 minutes and overshadowed Sam Etcheverry, the famous rifle-armed Als quarterback. Eskimos felt they could effectively defuse the Etcheverry bombs, just as they had done in 1954 and 1955, and again they were correct. Etcheverry had one of the most frustrating afternoons of his career. He completed only 15 of 38 aerials for 293 yards and had four passes intercepted.

Getty showed plently of poise and before he was finished with the befuddled, weak-tackling Als, he helped wreck all sorts of Cup records. But still, with all his cool efficiency, he moved over to make room for a superstar. It had to be Jackie Parker, who continued his habit of putting the boots to the Als. He beat them with an 85- yard touchdown in the 1954 final and had them going around in circles with his Houdini-like ball-handling in 1955.

This time, Parker demolished them—with Getty's help—and erased a couple of Cup records that first went into the books in 1913, just four years after Earl Grey donated his trophy for "amateur football." Parker scored three touchdowns, one on a pass from Getty, and the others on five- and seven-yard runs. He also boomed a 65-yard single for a 19-point afternoon, obliterating the scoring mark of 15 established by Ross Craig in Hamilton in 1913 and equalled by two Toronto Argonaut players—the late Lionel Conacher in 1921 and Red Storey in 1938.

His 19-point day was broken a couple of years later by a comparative unknown, quarter Jim Van Pelt of the Blue Bombers, but the 27,425 fans at Varsity Stadium on this slightly-overcast afternoon saw the 23-year-old at his all-round greatest. Parker picked up 129 yards on 19 rushing plays, punted 12 times and was a rock on defence.

And he provided last-minute thrills that broke up the game, sent a wildly-cheering mob into the end zone just to touch the Great One and left the scoreboard man so confused he posted the wrong score.

The board read 51-27, rather than 50-27, and spectators left the stadium convinced that this was the final score.

Adding to the general confusion was this little event: Someone stole the ball from Parker. Many of the Als had left the field and so did the man in charge of the footballs. That left Eskimos with no football to try the convert and the scoreboard man simply awarded Eskimos the extra point which, of course, was not legal.

Herb Trawick, Als' captain, reported to game officials that he couldn't find a ball and, after a fast conference with the Eskimos, officials said that was it. End of the ball game. Warren Stevens, director of athletics at the University of Toronto, later explained the scoreboard man's error this way: "He just got a little excited, as everyone was, and added six to 44 to make it 51."

Statisticians sorted out the records set and came up with these: Total points scored by both teams: 77. The highest total previously was in 1923 when Queen's University beat Regina Roughriders 54-0. Touchdowns by both teams: 11, seven by Eskimos (three for Parker, two for Getty and a pair for Johnny Bright) and four by Montreal (two for Hal Patterson, one each by Etcheverry and Pat Abbruzzi). The previous record was nine, which had stood since the Queen's-Regina engagement.

Yards rushing by both clubs: 639. Edmonton gained 448 yards, Montreal 191. The old mark was 566 yards set by Eskimos and Als in 1955. Yards rushing by one team: 488 by Eskimos. In addition, Eskimos became the first team from the West to win the Cup three straight years, the fourth club in the country to win three straight and Pop Ivy joined a couple of other coaches to make it three-for-three in consecutive years.

University of Toronto reigned from 1909-11, Queen's 1922-24 and Toronto Argonauts 1945-47. Billy Hughes coached the Queen's teams and Teddy Morris the Argos.

A tragic postscript to football was written two weeks after this 1956 game. The annual all-star Shrine contest was held in the West with proceeds going to help crippled children. A Trans-Canada—later known as Air Canada—plane returning to the East following the contest crashed into Mount Slesse in the Rockies.

The dead included Calvin Jones of Winnipeg and Mel Beckett, Mario DeMarco, Gordie Sturtridge and Ray Syrnyk, all of Saskatchewan Roughriders. The families of Beckett and DeMarco later donated

120

the Beckett-DeMarco Memorial Trophy, awarded annually to the out-standing lineman in the West.

This year, some fans wondered what ever became of the foot in foot-ball. Long-memoried statistical buffs recalled the good olds when Bummer Stirling, Lionel Conacher, Bob Isbister, Jr., Ab Box and many others regularly sent the football for long rides. The foot returned in 1957, probably the most celebrated in the game. And it didn't even belong to a player.

CHAPTER XXIII

THE WINNING JIM TRIMBLE

Nov. 30, 1957, at Toronto
Hamilton Tiger-Cats 32, Winnipeg Blue Bombers 7

Over the years, Hamilton picked up the reputation of producing rough, tough football clubs befitting a steel town. The system wasn't sophisticated, nothing like the Old School Tie aura that surrounded Toronto Argonauts, the Blues of the University of Toronto, the Tricolor of Queen's University or the Rough Riders of Ottawa.

It was something a little different than the roisterous, hard-hitting, fun-loving Toronto Balmy Beaches. Fans associated the Tabbies with something along the lines of legalized mayhem. Likely as not these kindly assassins would stumble over their own feet if they tried to dazzle the opposition with footwork. On offence, it was a case of brute force as exemplified by one of the most feared men in the game—Brian Timmis, the Old Man of the Mountain who disdained headgear when he barrelled over opposing linemen in the 1920s and 1930s.

This tradition stayed with the club. It wasn't particularly elegant to watch, but the offensive unit could rely on the defensive squad to clasp opponents aganst hairy bosoms until their eyeballs popped. The trouble was that Hamilton's style of play didn't produce big scores. Or, as their sensitive fans had been pointing out lately, it didn't get the team into the Grey Cup final with a consistency they demanded. And the immediate prospect of a Tiger-Cat club getting another shot at Earl Grey's trophy wasn't bright.

Montreal Alouettes, who lived, and died, with the pass were the unquestioned rulers in the East. Tiger-Cats did make it to the Cup final in 1953 and managed a 12-6 victory over the pass-happy Winnipeg Blue Bombers. The Als, with Sam Etcheverry pulling the trigger, picked holes in the opposing defences and, although beaten three straight by Edmonton Eskimos in the Cup final starting in 1954, they certainly weren't showing signs of falling apart.

Jake Gaudaur, who centred and captained the newly-born Tiger-Cat club in 1950 and was a formidable cog in the 1953 machine, moved up to become the club's president. He decided after the 1955 season that maybe the Tabbies were geting a little flabby. It was time, he felt, to put some more muscle in the club. Jake was impressed with the rough-house play of Philadelphia Eagles in the National Football League and he was on the doorstep when they fired Head Coach Jim Trimble. The rap against Trimble, said Eagle officials, was that "he was too tough on the players."

Gaudaur hired him in 1956 to succeed Carl Voyles. The talkative six-foot-two 250-pounder was an immediate hit and Hamilton fans loved it when he summed up his feeling about football in one short sentence: "It's like war." They had latched on to this square-jawed man who once worked at a steel mill in his home town of McKeesport, near Pittsburgh, who sang tenor in his church choir at Aldershot, just outside Hamilton, helped organize strawberry festivals, took part in heavy scrimmages to show his hirelings how it was done. And, more to the point, he was willing to settle it with fists with any player who challenged his authority.

Moreover, he was a delight to football writers. "Hell," he once said, "I don't know if I'm the highest-paid coach in the country, but I ought to be. I'm the best coach in the country." He had a captive audience and, caught up with enthusiasm, he amended his statement to read: "I'm the best damned coach in North America."

Disbelievers lined up four abreast in 1956 when Montreal beat Tiger-Cats 30-21 and 48-41 in the Eastern final. Trimble watched the Eskimos annihilate Alouettes 50-27 in the Cup and was convinced that the only way to beat the West—specifically the Eskimos—was to put together the roughest, toughest bunch of players he could gather.

He had made a start. In 1956, he picked up Cookie Gilchrist and Ralph Goldston to go with tough, hard Vince Scott, Eddie Bevan and others. In 1957, he hit the jackpot when he signed John Barrow, one of the finest tackles and middle guards in the country. Also, this year, Ticats signed Bernie Faloney, the smooth quarterback from Maryland who had called the shots when Edmonton beat Alouettes 26-25 in 1954. But things didn't change much during the regular season. Ticats scored only 250 points and had 189 scored against them, both lowest in the East, over their 14-game league schedule.

This was the old, familiar story. But, suddenly, Ticats got hot, socked it to the Als 39-1 in the second game of the two-game total-point Eastern final to win the series 56-11. Controversial Jim Trimble's vocal chords were well oiled and he did not disappoint. Meanwhile, Winnipeg's miracle Bombers stunned the Eskimos in a wild, heart-stopping best-of-three Western final that went the limit.

The Bombers, who finished the league schedule in second place, four points behind Eskimos, ran the experts underground with a first-game 19-7 victory at home. They lost the second 5-4 at Edmonton and locked up a Grey Cup berth with a 17-2 triumph at Edmonton in a fierce game that took two 10-minute overtime periods to settle after the clubs were deadlocked 2-2 in regulation time. The Bombers relied on a magnificent defence, allowing the fast-striking Eskimos only one touchdown in 200 minutes of play.

A personal touch was added to the Cup buildup. Trimble's opposite number was Bud Grant, who had played for Philadelphia Eagles when Trimble was their coach. The rangy end had gone to Bombers as a player and this was his rookie year as coach. Trimble listened to the experts talk of the great defensive battle that fans at Varsity Stadium would watch in the Cup final and pointed out that they were nuts.

"Those guys (Bombers) will have to score 30 points to beat us," he predicted. The scoreboard made him a genius. But Westerners weren't impressed. That kind of stuff is for teacup readers, they said. And they justifiably pointed out that Bombers should have made the trip to Toronto in a hospital car. They had a long list of injuries after the Edmonton series and it lengthened in the head-knocking against Ticats.

The Bombers were hurt badly early in the game and Western writers and fans said a healthy Winnipeg club could have taken Tiger-Cats. Big Jim termed this "bellyaching" and climbed out on another limb. He was coach of the Eastern All-Stars against the Western All-Stars in the Shrine game for charity the following week at Montreal and made another prediction: "We'll win by three touchdowns."

The scoreboard read: East 20, West 2: exactly three unconverted touchdowns. If not much else, it made Jim Trimble No. 1 on the most-despised list of Western Canada football fans.

But back to the Cup final: Ticats celebrated with champagne, Ray (Bibbles) Bawel of Ticats with shoe polish on his ankle, the Canadian Rugby Union with egg on its face and a Toronto lawyer, who shall remain anonymous, with a mischievous twinkle in his eye.

The Bombers? They didn't have much left in this one. Gerry James, the West's scoring champion and son of one-time Regina Roughrider great, Eddie (Dynamite) James, suffered a broken finger on his right hand in the opening minutes. He ended the game with four key fumbles charged against him. Altogether, Bombers bobbled six times and recovered only one.

Punter Charlie Shepard retired in the first quarter with a gimpy leg. Quarterback Kenny Ploen followed him to the sidelines in the third with an injured left knee and Pete Mangum's injured knee wouldn't stand up. He watched most of the game from the bench.

The robust Ticats took advantage of every Winnipeg error—and, just as important, they made the Bombers commit errors and fumbles with their mauling, clawing, gang-tackling type of game. They creamed every ball carrier and it was apparent to the crowd of 27,349 and the chaps in the gold and blue uniforms that Bombers were in for a brutal afternoon. Cookie Gilchrist set the pattern nearly. He smeared halfback Dennis Mendyk who was dashing down the sidelines and the ball squirted into Bawel's arms at the Bomber 53. Result: Ticat touchdown No. 1 at 6:15 of the first quarter.

Less than three minutes later, Bob Hobert fumbled and Bernie Faloney finished off an 11-play march with a touchdown from the six. That was all the scoring until the fourth when Ticats added three more touchdowns—two by Gilchrist and one by Gerry McDougall—all on running plays. Bombers got their touchdown, a 15-yard pass from Barry Roseborough to Mendyk, with less than two minutes remaining in the game.

But the game's most spectacular play—unrehearsed and unprecedented in the long history of the Cup—was made with five minutes left to play and Tiger-Cats ahead 25-0. It brought abuse to the long-suffering CRU and eventually resulted in a gift of a $150 wrist watch to Bawel. Bawel had grabbed off a Winnipeg pass and took off for a certain touchdown. A fan, standing on the sidelines directly beside a policeman, put out a well-polished boot and the Ticat sprawled on his face at the Winnipeg 42.

Here was a setting for an old-fashioned rumble, undoubted blood-letting and an arrest. But nothing of consequence happened. Bawel scrambled to his feet, streaked back to the spot where the spectator was still standing and gave him a verbal going-over. Other Ticats charged over but with their big lead and the game out of reach of the Bombers, they confined their anger to some indignant cussing. A minute later, the spectator sauntered back to the vicinity of his field seat and was last seen heading for the exits.

Bawel displayed proof of the trip later in the Hamilton dressing room. It was a shoe-polish smear on his left ankle. Months after the game—so the story goes—Bawel received a tangible reminder of the incident. An associate of the tripper revealed that "the guy had conscience trouble" and sent the watch to Bawel at this home in Evansville, Ind. Inscribed on it were these words: "From The Tripper. Grey Cup, 1957."

The CRU, which had put in field seats for this game and had publicly warned spectators that they would be arrested on the spot if they interfered with play in any way, took abuse from fans for not affording maximum protection. And this was to be the last Cup final handled by the long-suffering Union. The Canadian Football League was to take over full control and operation of the game in 1958. It. too, was to be rapped for fan interference in later year.

Trimble? Every football fan in the West was after his hide. He had started what amounted to almost total war between Winnipeg and Hamilton, but no one can say he didn't liven up the football scene. Big Jim didn't win another Grey Cup, but that didn't stop him from talking. And, it seemed, every time he opened his mouth, a Westerner was ready to plant his foot in it. He probably should have kept quiet while he was ahead in the prediction department. He was fair game for some terrific letdowns and, to his credit, he kept bouncing up off the floor talking.

CHAPTER XXIV

THE AMATEUR EXIT

Nov. 29, 1958, at Vancouver
Winnipeg Blue Bombers 35, Hamilton Tiger-cats 28

It took 48 years, but the Big Four and Western Conference at last took the final, decisive step to sweep the amateurs under the rug and out of hearing. To be precise, it happened on a bitterly-cold, blustery day at the Bessborough Hotel in Winnipeg on Jan. 17, 1958.

The pros formed their own long-talked-about Canadian Football League, appointed G. Sydney Halter, a 52-year-old moustached Winnipeg lawyer, as their commissioner. From that day on, the CFL would run its own show on rule changes, import quotas, organization and operation of the Grey Cup final and all other matters concerning its own affairs. Nearly two months later, March 14, at an acrimonious, name-calling, closed-door session in the Royal York Hotel in Toronto, the CFL rubber-stamped everything it had decided in Winnipeg. But not before at least one punch was thrown in anger.

No longer would the Ontario Rugby Football Union, the Maritimes, Quebec and Intercollegiate Unions have a say in the affairs of the pros. The CFL got around this easily—it simply took the necessary two-thirds (10 of 15) voting control of the CRU when the Quebec and Maritime Unions deserted their amateur compatriots and voted with the CFL. The CFL was the supreme boss. It had the power to make changes in the CRU constitution without enlisting the support of the minor unions.

The ORFU, a one-time proud league whose clubs battled the Big Four and Western Conference on even terms on the field but in recent years was reduced to the status of farm clubs for the pros, raised a terrific fuss. But it knew its days as a power in football were gone.

ORFU spokesmen pointed out that the Grey Cup was donated for "amateur rugby" by Earl Grey in 1909 and thus, they argued, the pros had no legal right to compete for it, let alone take it over. They tried to win the Quebec and Maritimes league delegates to their side and lost. They threatened to take their case to the courts, but never did. They had been out of the Grey Cup picture for three consecutive years and they knew that all hope of at least a meeting on the field against the pros was gone.

Tempers became somewhat frayed and during one night session an ORFU delegate came out swinging when a Western official made derogatory remarks about the union. "The guy didn't even have the courtesy to hold his tongue when he knew that we were beaten at the conference table," an ORFU official later told a reporter. "There was no reason to rub it in and he would have taken a pasting if people didn't stop our guy." When the fuss had died down spokesmen for the pros were quick to declare that the steps taken were in the best interests of football.

"I'm definitely satisfied that the best interests of junior and intermediate football in Canada have been served by the decisions taken," Halter said. "We were prepared to withdraw from the CRU if we didn't win the increased vote," he added. "We didn't want this to happen because it would do harm to the CRU. The only reason the members of the Canadian Football League remained within the framework of the CRU was our desire to assist junior and intermediate football in any manner.

"If we had pulled out the men behind these groups might have lost interest in the game and the CRU almost definitely would fall apart. We are still prepared to subsidize the CRU for the development of minor football." The break was complete—the pros ran their show, the amateurs theirs—but there was one small detail to be settled: The trophy.

The CRU held onto it until June, 1966, when the Union officially turned it over to the CFL. Bill McEwen of Ottawa, CRU president, announced at a special general meeting that the CRU as such was going out of business on Jan. 1, 1967, to be reborn as the Canadian Amateur Football Association. "As a last gesture before the name change, the Grey Cup, which has been in the custody of the CRU since its presentation . . . in 1909, was turned over to the Canadian Football League to be held in trusteeship by the president and the secretary of the CFL," McEwen said. "Our objective is to become the true governing body of all amateur football in Canada."

The last chapter was written of the CRU story. The Union was established in 1882 to promote amateur football in Canada. It had suffered through many years of bickering with East and West over rule changes, import rules, Grey Cup operation and other related problems.

It wasn't alone. East and West committee-room battles were commonplace through the years. Football men could not see eye to eye on many issues and obstinate thinking ruled out East-West Grey Cup confrontations a couple of years.

Suddenly, in 1948, it struck the pros that they had the greatest sports spectacle in the country in their hands when Calgary Stampeders and their fun-loving, uninhibited fans barrelled into Toronto and blew the town apart with good-natured and colorful pre-game antics. It was time to pull the knives out of backs and get down to constructive thinking. East and West got together and piece by piece built the foundation for one all-embracing pro league with full autonomy of its operation. It took 10 tough years to accomplish.

Meanwhile, in 1958, Hamilton Tiger-Cats went about the business of getting to the Cup final and to prove that their 1957 triumph was no steal. They stayed with much the same personnel but Coach Jim Trimble proudly proclaimed they were 25 per cent stronger than the previous year. The Bombers? Well, they more or less stayed pat but they did sign a fellow named James Sutton Van Pelt, a 23-year-old Chicago-born Dutchman who had quarterbacked the University of Michigan.

The Bombers, however, still had Kenny Ploen to call the signals. So, maybe, this young newcomer could be labelled excess baggage. But the Bombers encountered problems early in the season. Ploen was injured. Gerry James was sidelined with a broken leg and coach Bud Grant solved the problem by inserting Van Pelt as quarterback and placement kicker. Ploen returned, but as a halfback. Tiger-Cats whipped through the East schedule with a 10-3-1 record and walloped Ottawa Rough Riders 35-7 and 19-7 in the two-game total-point final.

Bombers ended their schedule with a 13-3 record, got past Edmonton Eskimos in the best-of-three Western playoff by 30-7, 7-30 and 23-7 scores. And they were healthy. "Everybody's in good shape," said Coach Bud Grant. What now, Jim Trimble? "Well," said Jim, "we think we'll win. Our club is 25 per cent better than it was last year and, besides, we've spotted definite weaknesses in the Winnipeg team we think we can exploit."

Maybe Ticats did find some Bomber weaknesses but when the teams walked off the field just about everyone agreed that this was the toughest, best-played Cup final in years and that the best team won. The thumping that went on at Empire Stadium was indicated in the statistics—eight fumbles, four by each team, and 16 penalties, 10 of these against Ticats for 97 yards.

And rookie Jimmy Van Pelt dazzled old pro Bernie Faloney, Hamilton's quarterback. Van Pelt scored a Cup record 22 points on two touchdowns, two field goals and four converts, completed nine of 17 forwards and carried the ball four times for 28 yards, including a one-yard over-centre plunge in the fourth quarter that wiped out a 28-27 Hamilton lead.

His first touchdown, in the opening quarter, came on a play that Easterners probably had never seen before. With Bombers in possession on the Tiger-Cat 29-yard line, Van Pelt pitched out to Leo Lewis and streaked down the sidelines to take a forward from Lewis without a Ticat laying a hand on him.

There were other Blue Bomber heroes. Defensive end Norm Rauhaus, a fine, young Canadian, set no records but he showed up in the statistics with a vital blocked punt that he turned into a touchdown on the final play of the opening half. And he made a key interception in his own end zone to halt a late Tiger-Cat drive. The other Winnipeg touchdown came in the third quarter on a two-yard plunge by Charlie Shepard. Gerry McDougall and Ron Howell each scored a pair of Hamilton touchdowns. McDougall rambled over on a nine-yard play and a two-yard plunge and Howell caught two Faloney end-zone passes.

Ralph Goldston scored the other—a 65-yard gallop in the opening quarter after picking up a Van Pelt fumble. Steve Oneschuk kicked the converts. Goldston gained some degree of notoriety on the last play of the second quarter when umpire Taylor Paterson of Regina caught him planting a fist in Leo Lewis' face. Goldie, a crunching defensive halfback and a sometime ball carrier on offence, was tossed out of the game. Trimble thought the penalty was too severe. "I think any roughing penalty would have sufficed—15 yards for roughing or 15 yards for a personal foul."

But he was quick to point out that Goldston's ejection "didn't lose the ball game for us. Winnipeg certainly deserved to win. We have no alibis." Blue Bomber players agreed almost to a man that "Trimble's big mouth gave us the incentive to win" and as the teams left the field some Western fans in the stands chanted to the tune of Tom Dooley: "Hang down your head, Jim Trimble, hang down your head and cry. Hang down your head, Jim Trimble, you've got to eat humble pie." Jim Trimble did, indeed. But he was back in a year—still talking.

CHAPTER XXV

BLUE BOMBER PAY DIRT

Nov 28, 1959, at Toronto
Winnipeg Blue Bombers 21, Hamilton Tiger-Cats 7

Bud Grant hit Canada at a time when Blue Bombers and Montreal Alouettes were passing the ball about with great abandon. The theory seemed to be that if you threw it often enough you were sure to win. Spectators loved those golden arms of Sam Etcheverry of the Als and Indian Jack Jacobs of the Bombers and they were filling the parks. Sam and Jake were past masters in the art of sending the football for long aerial rides.

But there was one flaw. Great throwing arms, nifty pass-catching ends such as Bud Grant who joined Bombers in 1953 after two years with Philadelphia Eagles of the National Football League, weren't winning the Grey Cup. They were picking up great yardage in the East-West classic—between the goal lines. In 1953, for instance, Indian Jack uncorked a Cup record 46 passes, completed 28. The Bombers lost to the Hamilton Tiger-Cat ground troops.

In 1954-1955-1956 the air was full of footballs, as they say, when Etcheverry and friends visited Big Four stadiums in Toronto, Hamilton and Ottawa. The pass got Als to the Cup finals and Sam was still in rare pitching form but that old tuck-it-in-the-belly and ram down the middle, slice off-tackle or whip around the ends by Edmonton Eskimos was a little bit better. The bread-and-butter plays were the ball-carrying junkets.

Edmonton Eskimos and their split-T double-fullback formation won out each time. It didn't shoot the spectators out of their seats in great glee because hardly anyone, including the opposition, was sure where the football was. And when you get only occasional glimpses of the ball when Eskimos were in possession, what is there to yell about?

It may have been lacklustre football, but it sent Eskimos to the top of the Western Conference standings each year, victories in the

131

playoff and a place in the Cup final. All these years Grant was catching passes for Bombers under the coaching of Allie Sherman who went to New York Giants after the 1956 season. The Blue Bomber executive chose 30-year-old prematurely-grey Grant to take over the coaching job in 1957.

The year previous, president Jake Gaudaur of Tiger-Cats had decided the only way to stay in line with the Eskimos—and beat the Als—was to get a rough, tough coach who would beef up the defensive corps with a bunch of roughnecks. Grant had played for Jim Trimble, the one-time Eagles coach, and he knew, too, that firepower along the ground, plus a quarterback who could throw, and a crisp, tough, quick-striking defensive unit was the key to the Grey Cup strongbox.

The similarity between the two coaches ended there. Trimble, always talking and always selling football, didn't think twice about peeling the skin off any player who pulled a rock. Grant, the original silent man, was cool, calculating and rarely—if ever— showed emotions while standing ramrod straight on the sidelines.

He knew football. He knew, too, that the foot belonged in the Canadian game. He had just the man for the quick kick in this 1959 Cup final. Fullback Charlie Shepard kicked singles as fast as he had the opportunity. As if his orthodox punting weren't enough, he turned the Cats around galloping after the bouncing ball with four quick kicks on second down. Most of Shepard's damage was inflicted in a wild 10 minutes of the fourth quarter when he scored 10 points in just over 11 minutes on a touchdown and four singles. His rampage put Tiger-Cats out of reach and, just to make sure, Bombers added another touchdown with only 20 seconds remaining in the game.

For the capacity crowd of 33,133 in the Canadian National Exhibition stadium the fourth quarter provided the fireworks of a scoring spectacle the chilled fans wanted. On the slippery, soggy playing field the teams had fought 40 minutes in a bitter but colorless struggle for points that came the hard way. One quick thrust by Bombers in the opening minutes of play paved the way for a 21-yard field goal by Gerry James. A blocked kick—on a play that will long be talked about—gave Ticats a single point in the second quarter.

The third period was half over before Tiger-Cats squeezed into a lead. On third down from the Winnipeg two-yard line Hamilton elected to go for a field goal instead of the inviting touchdown. Steve Oneschuk kicked the three-pointer from the 10-yard line and with only 14

132

seconds of the quarter left he kicked another, this time from 27 yards, and Hamilton carried a 7-3 lead into the final 20 minutes.

The shiny dream of Hamilton supporters turned into a nightmare. Robert Porter Tinsley, 35-year-old lineman of the Blue Bombers, draped his 268-pound hulk over a fumbled ball by Gerry McDougall of Tiger-Cats and the Cup hopes of Hamilton were squashed. In the 10 minutes after the bobble, the Bombers had struck for 18 points. Shepard plunged over for his touchdown after a 40-yard pass from quarter Kenny Ploen to Farrell Funston put the ball on the Hamilton three and, with the game in the bag, Ploen hit Ernie Pitts with a 33-yard TD in the final seconds.

The defensive play of the two clubs was somewhat awesome. They gained a net total of 216 yards rushing—129 by Winnipeg and 87 by Hamilton. Quarter Bernie Faloney threw all but two of Ticat's 23 passes which produced only 10 completions and 93 yards. Ploen took to the air 10 times and Halfback Leo Lewis once and they connected four times for 104 yards.

The post-mortems centred around the blocked kick in the second quarter. Play was on the Winnipeg 18 and Shepard dropped back to punt. Vince Scott of Ticats burst through the Winnipeg line, blocked the kick and followed the ball into the end zone along with a flock of Bomber and Ticat players. Scott dove for the ball and both he and the ball kept sliding and it got away from him. Jack Delveaux of the Bombers fell on it.

Referee Paul Dojack said that Scott never had possession, that the ball went past him. Jake Gaudaur said Scott had momentary possession and, under the rules, that called for a touchdown. Whatever it was, and what really mattered to the Bombers was that they had beaten Tiger-Cats in two of three meetings. Grant was to win another pair over Trimble in 1961 and 1962.

Within years, both men were back in the NFL. Trimble joined New York Giants in 1966 as an assistant coach and Grant moved into the head coach's job with Minnesota Vikings on March 13, 1967. In head-to-head Cup meetings, Grant was the clear-cut winner with four of five victories. Off the field, though, Trimble left Grant a distant second in verbiage—by a few million words. But then talk didn't win Grey Cups.

133

CHAPTER XXVI

THE VANCOUVER RIOTS

Nov. 26, 1960, at Vancouver
Ottawa Rough Riders 16, Edmonton Eskimos 6

Harry McBrien went to the 1953 Grey Cup final in a hearse with a motorcycle police escort. He rode in a taxi from the site of the game to his hotel carrying nothing more than an empty box and was escorted every yard of the way by three grim policemen who thought he was carrying around a fortune.

He was a timer in some of the biggest fight cards in Toronto and an official in international track and field meets. He had enough kicks and thrills to last an average sports official a lifetime. But none of this compared with this Nov. 26 Saturday afternoon at Empire Stadium in Vancouver. This was the day that Harry stood out like a beacon as thousands of wild fans tumbled out of their seats and onto the field, tore down goalposts and forced an unprecedented halt to the Cup final. The scoreboard showed 41 seconds left to play.

One young man nonchalantly walked between Ottawa and Edmonton players, picked up the game ball and vanished in the mob on the field that had increased to about 5,000 persons. The ball-stealer was the most prominent person on the field. But who could have missed a nearly-bald man, his coat-tails flying in the breeze, yelling at the top of his voice and frantically giving the choke-up sign? It was Harry McBrien, ordinarily a placid individual who met crises head-on with a wide grin, a twinkle in his always-smiling eyes, a shrug and a joke. But this wasn't the time to stand back and think things over.

He was the only person, apart from the players and game officials, who had a right to be on the playing field. As Grey Cup co-ordinator and right-hand man of Commissioner G. Sydney Halter of the Canadian Football League, Harry was errand boy for many of the jobs involved in staging the East-West sawoff. He handled the thankless job of ticket distribution. He arranged the half-time entertainment and hundreds of other chores and he always came up smiling.

There were nearly 75 policemen at the game who spent most of their time cooling out drunks and stopping fights, but they did not do much when the mob started to pour out of the end zones and onto the field. That is, until Harry got into the action. A policeman spotted him, put an arm on Harry and stopped his mad dash. Probably any other football official in the land would have used strong-man methods of his own, but not Harry.

Let him tell it: "I'm standing on the sidelines with the commissioner when that mob was running all over the place and I turn to him and say: 'We've gotta do something.' Under the circumstances, that has to be the understatement of the century. The commissioner doesn't bat an eye and says: 'Okay, call it off.' Just like that. I go tearing out onto the field and what do you know? A cop is trying to keep me off and I'm the only guy on the field any policeman is stopping. So I say 'the hell with you' and wave him off. I can't get within 20 yards of Seymour Wilson (referee from Hamilton) so I eventually catch his eye and with all my screaming, and yell 'call it off' and give him the choke-up sign.

"Seymour got the message okay and waved the players off the field." There's more to his story. He was busy at the stadium long after the 36,592 fans and players had departed. "At last I'm all cleaned up and there isn't a taxi in sight. I order one from downtown and shortly after, this cab—mine—pulls up. The commissioner stepped into it, not knowing of course that it was mine, and away it goes."

Harry had been secretary of the Canadian Rugby Union and the pros grabbed him when the CFU took over operation of the Cup final in 1958. He had been doing the same job with CRU. The 1960 incident by the destructive and unruly field-invading spectators was something new and not a bit hilarious to Harry McBrien and other football officials. "The police invited this thing," stormed Halter. "They did absolutely nothing. They might have been cardboard dummies out there."

Gordon Wynn, president of the Eskimos, termed the spectacle "the most disgraceful exhibition I've ever seen" and Lew Hayman, general manager of Toronto Argonauts, said he was "ashamed by the whole thing." There was talk that the CFL might have second thoughts about awarding Vancouver the East-West final again, but it was back again in 1963 and again in 1966 and each created some controversy. In 1963,

135

big Angelo Mosca of the Hamilton Tiger-Cats was charged with deliberately piling on fleet Willie Fleming of British Columbia Lions and in 1966 hoodlums turned downtown Vancouver streets into a battleground of sorts on the eve of the game.

Back to 1960. The game demonstrated that few plays in football can be as devastating as a lost fumble or as effective as a fumble recovery. Rough Riders turned Eskimo fumbles into 10 points—a first-quarter 15-yard field goal by Gary Schreider following a fumble by halfback Rollie Miles of the Eskimos and a final-quarter touchdown by guard Kaye Vaughan who fell on the loose ball in the Edmonton end zone after a bobble by Joe-Bob Smith of the Eskimos. The clubs traded second-quarter touchdowns on passes by old pro Jackie Parker of Edmonton and rookie Russ Jackson of the Riders who had taken over the signal-calling from Ron Lancaster.

Parker caught end Jim Letcavits on a 65-yard pass-and-run TD midway through the period and Jackson put Riders ahead 9-6 two minutes later on a 31-yard pass to Bill Sowalski. Schreider kicked the convert. Eskimos threatened late in the game following a 77-yard dash down the sidelines by Parker but two key interceptions by Joe Poirier and Doug Daigneault and a fumble recovery wiped out their scoring chances. The Daigneault interception came with less than three minutes remaining in the game and set the stage for the fan disturbance. It was second-and-seven with Riders in possession on their own 33 when the first horde of fans surged onto the field, preventing further play.

CFL officials pondered the situation and all were agreed on one thing: If the game had been close and Eskimos had a chance of winning when the rumpus started, the CFL would have had a riot on its hands. The players, themselves, probably sensing that any rough stuff at this time would have created an ugly situation, stood around watching the wild mob scene.

Rough Riders players tempered their wild exhilaration about beating the 3½-point favorite Eskimos, including well-known East spoiler Jackie Parker, with some misgivings of their own. They complained about the players' share of the receipts—$500 to each member of the winning team and $300 to each loser—and they resented some critics' published reports that Riders were the second-best football club in the East.

"Look at it this way," explained team captain Bobby Simpson about the Cup payoff. "I'm losing money in the Cup final. And so are a lot of other guys on this club. I have a contract that pays me much

136

Les "Butch" Lear, an old side-kick of the late Ches McCance of great Winnipeg clubs in the late 1930s and early 1940s, played for and coached Calgary Stampeders to a shattering 12-7 victory over Ottawa Rough Riders in 1948. That victory sent Canadian football into the wildest spending spree of any sport in the country.

Alexandra Studios

Incomparable Joe (King) Krol (left) with Bob Sandberg, Winnipeg Blue Bomber quarterback, after the Toronto Argonaut's stirring 10-9 Grey Cup victory in 1947. Krol, one of the finest Canadian-born players, still holds the all-time Grey Cup scoring record with 30 points.

A Toronto, or is it a Winnipeg?, player watches in dismay as the ball heads for a landing in the slop in the famous 1950 Mud Bowl at Varsity Stadium in Toronto. The Toronto Argonauts won the Grey Cup with a 13-0 decision over the Winnipeg Blue Bombers.

Toronto Telegram

Jackie Parker loves that Cup! The Mississippi Magic Man led The Edmonton Eskimos to three straight Cup titles over Montreal Alouettes in 1954, 1955 and 1956.

Hamilton Spectator

Out of focus? No, the photographer snapped just as Charlie Shephard of Winnipeg Blue Bombers caught a touchdown pass while Don Sutherin (22) of Hamilton Tiger-Cats moved in too late. This was one of many scoring plays most of the 32,655 fans did not see in the 1962 Fog Bowl at the CNE Stadium in Toronto. Winnipeg won 28-27 in the two-day Saturday-Sunday contest.

Above: Angelo Mosca of Hamilton Tiger-Cats (68) is about to land on fallen Willie Fleming of British Columbia Lions (15) in the second quarter of the 1963 Cup final at Vancouver. Thousands in the 36,465 crowd screamed foul, but game officials ruled that the 268-pound Mosca had committed himself on the play before Fleming was downed by Ticats' Joe Zuger. Fleming, who suffered a slight concussion and did not return to action, tries to get up (below). Hamilton won 21-10.

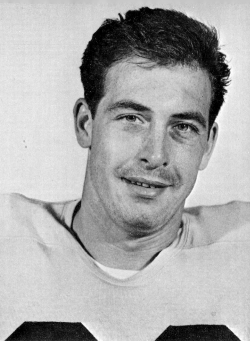

Canadian Press

*John Barrow (left) and Tommy Grant (right) of Hamilton Tiger-Cats have each play-
ed in nine Grey Cup finals, a record unmatched since Earl Grey donated the trophy
in 1909. All of their East-West games were played with the Ticats — in 1957, 1958,
1959, 1961, 1962, 1963, 1994, 1965 and 1967. Barrow, one of the greatest linebackers in the game, announced his retirement in 1970. Pass-catching Grant was traded
to Winnipeg Blue Bombers in 1969.*

*Jim Trimble, Hamilton Tiger-Cat coach (right) appears to ponder a remark by Bud
Grant, his counterpart with Winnipeg Blue Bombers, during one of their many Grey
Cup meetings. Actually, though, they are on opposite sides of the field and wired for
spotters' reports high up in the stands.*

Hamilton Spectator

Vic Washington, speedy 187-pound Ottawa halfback, takes off on 79-yard touchdown run after picking up his own fumble in the 1968 Ottawa-Calgary Grey Cup final at Toronto. Ottawa came from behind to defeat the Stampeders 24-21. (CP).

An Old Story: Coach Frank Clair of Ottawa Rough Riders is accustomed to these Grey Cup free rides. Here he is being chaired after the Riders beat Saskatchewan 29-11 in the 1969 final at Montreal. The victory was the fifth in the East-West classic for Clair, equalling a mark established by Lew Hayman.

Montreal Gazette

Prime Minister Pierre Elliott Trudeau presents the Grey Cup to Ottawa Rough Riders' Russ Jackson after Ottawa's 29-11 victory in 1969 over Saskatchewan Roughriders at Montreal.

more than the dough I get in the biggest game of all. We prove we're good enough to make it all the way to the Cup final, win it, and we take a cut in pay. What kind of a deal is that?" Other Rough Riders echoed his sentiments and they decided to do something about it. The players held meetings, formed their own chapter of the Canadian Football Players' Association and went after other clubs to join.

They met resistance in some quarters but in a few years all nine CFL rosters got together as a tightly-knit unit and the CFL finally agreed to a pre-season all-star game in 1970 with proceeds going to the Players' Association pension fund. Grey Cup payoffs also were increased—to $1,500 for each member of the winning team and $1,000 to each loser.

Riders were angry at well-publicized reports that they were the second-best team in the Big Four. These emanated from Toronto where the suddenly-revitalized Argonauts had finished on top of the standings, two points up on the Riders. Argos, the whipping boys in the East for years and destined to be easy pickings for at least five of the next six or seven seasons, had picked up quarterback Tobin Rote, said to be a washed-up refugee from the National Football League.

With Rote, it was a different ball game. Argos had never smelled the fresh, clean air of a first-place schedule-ending team since 1946 when they tied Montreal at the top. But 1960 was different. Argonauts, with Rote directing traffic, won 10 of 14 league games against Ottawa's 9-5 record. Rough Riders polished off Montreal 30-14 in the sudden-death semi-final, beat Toronto 33-21 to take a 12-point lead into the second game on Argo home grounds of the total-point Eastern final.

Argos boomed into a 20-0 lead midway through the third period. They had pushed Rough Riders all around the Canadian National Exhibition stadium and they were ahead 41-33 on the round. In the first half they allowed Ottawa to get inside Toronto territory only four times and the farthest Riders could penetrate was to the Argo 30. But the situation changed dramatically midway through the third quarter when Riders scored two touchdowns in 77 seconds. And in the fourth quarter Simpson made Argos look silly with the old-fashioned sleeper play.

As the crowd of 30,529 looked on in amazement, Simpson stayed close to the sidelines with Riders in possession on their own 12-yard line. Riders called a quick huddle, quarterback Ron Lancaster said only "it's a pass" to bewildered teammates and got away a long one to Simpson at the Toronto 40. Simpson galloped to the Toronto 18 where he was tackled, and in two plays Joe Kelly went over from the two-yard line for his second touchdown of the game. The six points put the game out of reach of Argonauts who held a wide statistical edge throughout the 60 minutes.

It was a 21-20 game victory and a 54-41 margin on the round. Many of the Rough Rider players on the bench didn't know what was going on out there and Simpson, a colorful character in and out of uniform, tossed an amazed Coach Frank Clair a big wink as he chugged past the Rider bench. It was the last sleeper play seen in Canadian pro football. On Feb. 11, 1961, the CFL outlawed the play.

CHAPTER XXVII

THE INCREDIBLE TRADE

Dec. 2, 1961, at Toronto
Winnipeg Blue Bombers 21, Hamilton Tiger-Cats 14
(overtime)

One telephone call set up a string of incidents that rocked Eastern pro football throughout the 1960s. In quick-fire succession it: produced the most spectacular trade in Canadian football history; reduced the once-proud Montreal Alouettes to a pathetic also-ran for 10 years; gave Hamilton Tiger-Cats an air of respectability, power and affluence after a one-year decline, and confirmed Jake Gaudaur as the most astute official in the game.

The Als, a power since 1953 and three-straight Grey Cup finalists—1954-56—suddenly found themselves in the same boat with Toronto Argonauts, the pushovers of the Big Four. Ticats, after a dreadful last-place Big Four finish in 1960, made it to the Cup final every year in the next five.

Jake? He was finally talked into taking over as commissioner of the Canadian Football League in 1968. He was the man the CFL wanted when Commissioner G. Sydney Halter of Winnipeg announced he would retire Jan. 1, 1967, but Jake had things to clean up in Hamilton and wasn't available—just yet.

The significance of the phone call was pointed up in November, 1960, when it became obvious that the situation around Montreal Alouette headquarters was indeed explosive. Light a match in the immediate vicinity and the place would blow up, some wags suggested. This wasn't idle banter or gossip or rumor. Two incidents were proof. The first occurred on a rainy Sunday night at Dorval Airport in Montreal after the team's return following a losing game. It was reported that coach Perry Moss ordered an immediate workout and Hal Patterson, one of the finest pass-catching ends and an unusually placid person, balked at the idea. The two men had words. The next came after the Als, who finished the regular schedule in third place, were beaten

30-14 by Ottawa Rough Riders in the Big Four sudden-death semi-final. Moss apparently chewed out quarterback Sam Etcheverry who had not thrown a pass in the first half.

This, indeed, was remarkable because Sam had lived by the pass in the league for years. He protested he had a sore arm. Football officials complained about this public washing of dirty linen. They wagged their heads and clacked their tongues and promptly put the odorous situation out of mind. Let owner Ted Workman, Moss, Patterson and Etcheverry work out their own little annoyances. Jake allowed the situation to nag at him for all of twenty-four hours. He had his own problems. He and a group of 11 Hamilton businessmen had bought the Tiger-Cat franchise in 1960 and it coincided with one of the club's worst seasons in years.

Vociferously vocal Ticat fans had been on quarter Bernie Faloney's back all year. The Cats had won only four of 14 games and had finished a demoralizing 12 points out of No. 1 position after three consecutive first-place finishes. This was not a time to sit around and think about his woes. Jake phoned Workman, discovered the Als owner was willing to talk trade and within hours the two were sitting in Workman's Montreal home.

They completed not one trade, but two. And, most important, there were no strings attached to the deals. They were unconditional trades. Workman let Patterson go for Don Paquette, a tough but undistinguished defensive end. Steal No. 1. And Etcheverry for Faloney, Steal No. 2 as subsequent events turned out. The Paquette-for-Patterson swap didn't pose any problems, But Etcheverry nixed his part of the deal. He had signed a secret contract with Workman saying he could not be traded without his consent.

Etcheverry interpreted the violated agreement as meaning he was a free agent. He would not report to Hamilton—instead, he said, he would sign with the National Football League's St. Louis Cardinals who had shown interest in him. Sam wasn't just talking. On Jan. 12, 1961, he signed a two-year contract with the Cards. The NFL approved it on Feb. 4 and there were murmurings that another CFL-NFL war was in the works. People had the wrong participants.

The battle was right in Montreal and it was all one-sided—Als fans against Workman. The Montreal owner was a loser all the way. The Als were without a quarterback, a first-string end and Workman could not come up with any sort of a plausible explanation for allowing such an outrageous situation to exist. The Als made it to the Big Four

148

final only once in the next 10 years and the league developed into two sections—Ottawa Rough Riders and the Ticats fighting for the top two spots with Als and Argos stringing along in the lower depths.

Before 1970 rolled around, ownership of the Als changed hands twice and attendance figures were alarming. Montreal was awarded a major-league baseball franchise that compounded Als patronage woes and the club, once one of the richest in the country, was considered a prime candidate for CARE.

Sam Etcheverry returned to the club in 1970 as head coach. Ticats enjoyed unprecedented success. They climbed to first place in 1961, held it every season through 1965, won the Grey Cup twice in that period—in 1963 and 1965—and, with an enlarged Civic Stadium, home-game attendance rose to an average of around 24,100 from 18,000.

The appearance of Patterson and strengthening in a couple of other spots worked wonders for Ticats in 1961. They ran away with the Big Four and were heading for a certain Grey Cup spot until they met the revitalized Argonauts in the two-game total-point final. Ticats made it in a real squeaker, and that was the end of serious Argo challenges for a few years.

Argos won the opener 25-7 at Toronto and, for the first time since 1952 when the club won the Cup, their fans could see no way they could lose out now. Ticat supporters were inclined to agree. But Argonauts did find a way, and a simple one at that. They forgot the foot was still in football. Ticats pushed Argos around Civic Stadium for nearly 58 minutes of the second contest and had evened the round score at 27-27 with Argos in possession on Hamilton's 29-yard line and the final seconds ticking away. The strategy called for a quick kick into the end zone stands, but someone on the club's board of strategy suffered a mental blackout.

Argos called for a running play, lost four yards and Dave Mann was forced to punt from outside the Hamilton 40. Tiger-Cats were well prepared. They positioned three men in the end zone, including Faloney. The ball went to him, he booted it back and in the ensuing confusion Faloney got the ball and ran for a touchdown, called back because of a rule infraction.

The game went into overtime. No contest. Ticats walked all over the confused Argos, won the game 48-2 and were ready to continue their Cup feud with Winnipeg Blue Bombers who had whipped Calgary 14-1 and 43-14 in the Western Conference two-of-three final. That is the way Bombers wanted it. They had beaten Ticats in 1958 and 1959 after losing in 1957 and they wanted nothing more than a chance to stuff what they termed Coach Jim Trimble's "big mouth" with another loss. They did it with some of the fiercest head knocking seen in a Cup final, although it took a little more than one period of overtime to give Coach Bud Grant his third Cup in four outings.

"We were beat up physically," Trimble told his players. "That Winnipeg was root-hogging, putting down their heads and charging. They're not very cute, but tougher than a boot." There was no doubt about that. The defensive unit—all-star tackle Frank Rigney, Roger Savoie, Herb Gray, Piper Cornell, George Druxman and backed up by Jack Delveaux, Dave Burkholder and other tough ones, held Ticats to only 25 yards rushing, 20 of them in the opening quarter.

The Bombers piled up 268 yards along the ground with Roger Hagberg and Leo Lewis doing most of the important rushing. The Ticats had the edge in the passing department—25 of 41 complete passes by Bernie Faloney against only 12 of 22 completions for Kenny Ploen and Hal Ledyard, who shared the Winnipeg quarterbacking. Tiger-Cats led 14-7 after three quarters but the game was forced into overtime— the only Cup final to go into extra time—on a three-yard third-quarter touchdown by Gerry James who accounted for 14 points on his touchdown, two converts and two field goals.

His touchdown tied it all up and, after a scoreless overtime period, Kenny Ploen drove over from 19 yards out for the winner, leaving Ticat tacklers strewn over the field as he took off down the sidelines. "It was supposed to be a drop-back pass on a hook pattern," he said. "I just ran out of the pocket—it's a bad habit I've got into."

Faloney uncorked his throwing arm for the two Hamilton touchdowns—a 90-yard pass-and-run play to Paul Dekker in the opening quarter and a 23-yarder to Ralph Goldston in the third. Don Sutherin, who later went to Ottawa Rough Riders, kicked the converts. Winnipeg's other point was kicked by Delveaux who had taken over from the injured Charlie Shepard.

This was the second 80-minute game in a week for Tiger-Cats, but they had no alibis for this loss. It probably wasn't the greatest of all Grey Cups, but it was close. As Coach Bud Grant of the Bombers mentioned to a Hamilton player en route to the dressing room: "It's a shame this one couldn't have ended in a tie."

150

CHAPTER XXVIII

THE FOG BOWL FIASCO

Dec. 1-2, 1962, at Toronto
Winnipeg Blue Bombers 28, Hamilton Tiger-Cats 27

A full-throated fan high up in the stands at the fog-bound Canadian National Exhibition waterfront stadium was yelling: "Only one thing left to do. Let's get down to some serious drinking." A spectator, easily identifiable as a Tiger-Cat supporter by the ribbons he was wearing, happened to spill a bag of popcorn in the face of another, who happened to be sporting the blue and gold of the Blue Bombers. The fist-swinging started and others in the vicinity started to choose partners when the police arrived and cooled out the belligerents.

"Well," yelled a Westerner, "how d'ya like that. It costs me five hundred bucks to come here this week and they break up the only action I can see."

To them, it seemed ironic that a person should have to pay up to $10 a seat to look at a huge bowl of fog being stirred around the lakefront. This was just the first instalment of the only football game in the history of the sport in North America to be played over a two-day period. The game was called on Saturday, Dec. 1, with nine minutes and 29 seconds to play because of fog, or invisible grounds. It was resumed at that point on Sunday afternoon with Bombers ahead 28-27 and in possession of the ball on the Hamilton 54-yard line and a second-and-10 situation.

It gave the coaches, Jim Trimble of Tiger-Cats and Bud Grant of the Bombers, 22 hours to plot strategy but the bright Sunday afternoon sun must have dazzled their heroes because it was a nothing-nothing game. This was the fifth Hamilton-Winnipeg Cup final in six years and, although Ticats had beaten the Westerners only once in this period, in 1957, Trimble again was in full voice. A few days before the game, Trimble sat in his office at Civic Stadium in Hamilton with Wilf

Gruson of The Canadian Press. The talk, naturally, was of Ticats' chances against the Bombers.

Trimble's comment produced probably the most widely-quoted statement of the year in Canadian football. "We'll uh, uh, waffle 'em," said the Tiger-Cat coach. "Yeah, that's it. We'll waffle 'em." "Waffle?" queried CP's football expert. "That's what I said," retorted Trimble. "You want me to keep telling people we'll beat 'em, or we'll whomp 'em? Do I hafta draw a picture so you guys can understand what I'm saying?"

No football fan needed a dictionary to find out what Big Jim had in mind. Not only that, but Jim gave Gruson the score: Hamilton 24 Winnipeg 12. And when the game ended after something like 25 hours, everyone knew that Trimble's Tiger-Cats did not waffle the Bombers. The spectators high up in the stands wouldn't know about that but it was obvious to the millions of television viewers who saw the action thanks to ground-level cameras.

The TV cameras played peek-a-boo with the players on the field but they did record all the scoring plays: Two touchdowns each for Leo Lewis and Charlie Shepard of the Bombers, a pair by Garney Henley and one each by Bobby Kuntz and Dave Viti of Ticats. Gerry James converted all four Bomber touchdowns while Don Sutherin of Ticats was good on only two extra-point tries and added a single in the third quarter on a wide field-goal attempt from 32 yards out. Two of the eight touchdowns were scored off passes. These were an end zone pitch to Shepard in the first quarter from Leo Lewis who had taken a handoff from quarter Hal Ledyard, and a 36-yard pass-and-run play from Joe Zuger to Viti in the third.

It was a rough afternoon for Sutherin, who later went to Ottawa Rough Riders and who hit the all-time Cup's big ten scorers in 1969. Those two missed converts and the attempted placement, if good, would have meant victory for the Eastern champions in regulation time. No one could fit him for goat horns. He was a rock on defence, just as he had been throughout the years for Tiger-Cats and, later, for Ottawa. It was an unfortunate afternoon for this one-time National Football League player with New York Giants and Pittsburgh Steelers who was an Eastern Conference all-star at defensive half in 1961 and again this year.

A crowd of about 15,000 turned out for the Sunday action compared with 32,655 on Saturday and many in the stands for the final

152

instalment must have wondered how Bombers managed to lead by a point. Throughout those nine minutes and 29 seconds they did not: Make a first down or gross a yard rushing and completed only one pass for four yards. Tiger-Cats gained 42 yards on the ground, completed four of eight passes for 63 yards. All the Bombers did was waffle Tiger-Cats for the fourth time in six years.

Of course, there was controversy. The fog had hardly lifted late Saturday when CFL Commissioner G. Sydney Halter was cornered. Why did he allow the game to go on as scheduled with that ominous fog coming in on the city? "I announced we were gambling strictly on the account that there were thousands of fans here from out of town who might not be able to stay another day to see the game," he said. "It was done because the weatherman assured me there would be no improvement the next day (Sunday) in the fog situation."

Was the decision to play influenced by the Canadian Football League's contract with the American Broadcasting Company which telecast the Cup final on its national network across the United States? "That is ridiculous," said Halter and Jake Gaudaur, CFL president. Jake, key figure in negotiating the contract with ABC, said the deal "had absolutely nothing to do with our decision." Purpose of the telecast, he said, was to get exposure of Canadian football in the U.S., and that the ABC crew had worked all Friday night editing film of the Montreal-Hamilton Eastern final for use in event the Cup final was postponed. "We'd have had U.S. exposure, anyway."

Halter emphasized that the final decision to call the game came after a delay of about 30 minutes. "This was not a committee decision. This was my decision as commissioner." U.S. exposure? Fog? Who cares? Certainly not Bud Grant.

It was Trimble's last appearance as a coach in Grey Cup play. In 1963 he went to Montreal Alouettes and Ralph Sazio took over. The pre-Grey Cup ballyhoo hasn't been the same since Big Jim left the scene.

Trimble, of course, had created all sorts of controversy before this 1962 game, but Calgary Stampeder players and their fans weren't listening. They were too shell-shocked following the final-game 12-7 loss in the best-of-three Western Conference final against Winnipeg. There have been some cliff-hangers through the years and this one ranks up there at the top.

Calgary had won the opener 20-14, lost the second 19-11 and led

7-6 in the rubber match with time remaining for only one play and Bombers lined up in field goal formation at the Stampeder 17. The Stamps put the big rush on, Gerry James' attempt was partially blocked by Jim Furlong, but the ball bounded into the Calgary end zone at the feet of Harvey Wylie with three Stampeders in pursuit. Harvey hesitated momentarily, kicked the ball soccer style as it lay on the ground and it smacked into Farrell Funston's stomach. The ball fell to the ground and Funston pounced on it with Wylie, Ernie Pitts and Frank Rigney of Bombers thrashing around.

It was a touchdown for Bombers. There was no convert attempt as swarms of spectators ganged onto the field at Winnipeg. If Wylie had fallen on the ball, the game would have been knotted 7-7 and overtime would be played.

If . . .

CHAPTER XXIX

THE ARGO DECLINE

Nov. 30, 1963, at Vancouver
Hamilton Tiger-Cats 21, British Columbia Lions 10

Lew Hayman couldn't go anywhere, except to the men's room, without some football fan heckling or commiserating with him over his so-sad Toronto Argonaut football team. He was stopped on the street. People phoned him at home and at his office and rarely could he go out to lunch without someone walking over to his table to give him advice.

Some people thought they should prefer charges of public mischief against the club. The incredible antics that Argos performed on the field were enough to call the cops. It wasn't that Argonauts were short of bodies to get the job done. They had some of the game's finest players but they couldn't put together 60 minutes of good football and, at their bumbling and missed-assignment best, it appeared that the boys in double blue uniforms were total strangers.

It was ironic to many supporters that this club, always well patronized at the gate and with a proud tradition behind it, could sink to the lower levels while British Columbia Lions should be battling this year for the biggest prize in Canadian football. The Lions were born in 1954 with a ready-made stadium in Vancouver, nothing more. They had made it to the Western Conference playoffs only once previously, in 1959, took a terrible beating from Edmonton Eskimos and from a fourth-place finish in 1962 moved into the No. 1 slot, won the Western playoffs and were ready to take on the Tiger-Cats.

The Argo decline really started after winning the Grey Cup in 1952. Four or five coaches later—Bill Swiacki, Lou Agase, Hamp Pool, Steve Owen, Nobby Wirkowski—and here they were out of contention after a couple of seasons when they came to life long enough to scare the wits out of Ottawa Rough Riders and Hamilton in the league playoffs. But those brief glory days were gone. Things had become so pitiful that some critics were saying that football to Argos was nothing much more than a spectator sport.

Argonauts placed last in the Eastern Conference from 1956 through 1959. And never once in those five years did they win more than four games a season. Old pro Tobin Rote from the National Football League gave them some degree of respectability as the 1960s opened, but he had fled back to the U.S. after the 1962 season and Argos were in a mess. Club officials always managed to put enough players in double blue uniforms for the inevitable slaughters and, many times, they must have wondered why they bothered.

Rote had moved them to a first-place finish in 1969 and it was life and death for Ottawa to get past them in the Eastern final. They finished third in 1961 and gave Hamilton a real scare in the post-season series. But, unfortunately for Argonauts, scares and near misses do not count. And 1962 was the same old story, four victories in 14 outings and a last-place finish.

Management would do anything short of kidnapping players to field a winner and in 1963, possibly after someone whispered a couple of big names in Hayman's ear, Argonauts negotiated a couple of deals. First they signed Jackie Parker of Edmonton Eskimos, a fellow who had an excellent reputation as an East spoiler in the big game and, incidentally, a box-office attraction. The magic man from Mississippi came expensive. To get him, Argos gave up five players and $15,000 cash.

Parker would be Toronto's leader. He would pull Argos up by the bootstraps, wrap the Grey Cup in tinsel and deposit it in Hayman's lap. But somewhere between Edmonton and Toronto that old winning formula had rubbed off the gimpy-legged quarterback-half. Argos finished the season with a 3-11 won-lost record, their worst since 1955. They signed Parker to a $25,000-a-year contract in February and, presto, it was money in the bank. Argonaut ads said "See Jackie Parker" and, indeed, fans did just that. The season ticket subscription list pushed close to 19,000 from the previous high of 18,000.

Argos' next deal was in the penny-ante class. Sandy Stephens, who quarterbacked the University of Minnesota Gophers to a Rose Bowl victory and was a high draft choice of National and American Football League clubs, was signed in 1962 by Montreal Alouettes for a reported $70,000 and they put him on waivers in September, 1963. Argos claimed him for the waiver price of $350. Als became disenchanted

156

with Stephens who they said, refused to trim down to 210 pounds from 225. Argos didn't mind paying up to a dollar a pound for a young fellow with potential. But it didn't pan out.

The Parker deal, made Feb. 12, was sandwiched between some others, involving coaches. Perry Moss was fired by Montreal in January. On Feb. 19, the Als signed Jim Trimble of Tiger-Cats to a three-year contract calling for $25,000 a year and a percentage of the gate receipts. The next day, Ralph Sazio, former Ticat tackle and latterly Trimble's assistant, moved into the head coach's chair.

"Now," said Trimble, "maybe Tiger-Cats can get a coach who can beat Bud Grant." The reference, of course, was to the Winnipeg Blue Bomber coach who had beaten Trimble and his 'Cats four times in five Cup meetings starting in 1957. But everybody, it seemed, was beating Grant and his Bombers this year. They ended in fourth place in the West and Sazio had to wait a couple of years to get at them.

Tiger-Cats, first in the East, beat Ottawa Rough Riders 63-35 in the two-game total-point series and the Lions, the big joke in the West for years, also finished first and defeated Saskatchewan Roughriders in the best-of-three final that went the limit. The Roughriders had stunned football fans across the country in their total-point series against Calgary. They lost the opener 35-9 in Calgary and back home, at Taylor Field in Regina, they whipped the Stampeders 39-12 to take the series 48-47.

Lions cooled them out in the final and the club that had to claw its way into the Western Conference 10 years ago was in its first East-West final.

The Lions weren't wanted in the Western Conference back in 1954 by Winnipeg and Saskatchewan because they feared B.C. would be a financial ball and chain. This year they were the most successful club around—on the field with only four losses, and at the bank. They had a young quarterback, 24-year-old Joe Kapp. His opposite number with Tiger-Cats was old pro Bernie Faloney, backed up by Joe Zuger and Frank Cosentino.

Tiger-Cats had Angelo Mosca, the 268-pound tackle whose favorite pastime was head-hunting. Big Angie enlivened the proceedings somewhat in the second quarter when he creamed Willie (The Wisp) Fleming, fleet Lions' back. Willie, streaking down the sidelines, was hit by Zuger and Mosca and watched the second half from the bench—in civvies. Thousands in the crowd of 36,545 at Empire Stadium screamed foul, claiming that Mosca had come in late and with Fleming lying on the turf and out of bounds.

No piling-on penalty was called. It was a judgment call and game officials ruled that Mosca had committed himself on the tackle before the B.C. speedster was downed by Zuger. Referee Ray Boucher of Ottawa checked with officials closest to the Fleming tackle—head linesman Tom Cheney and umpire Al Dryburgh—and they said there was no need for a penalty. That one play was game over for Lions who trailed 7-0 at the time. Even with a healthy Fleming it is doubtful that Lions could have won this one because Faloney was having one of his better days and the Ticat defensive unit with John Barrow, Mosca and company was keeping right in step.

Kapp completed 17 of 33 passes for 254 yards and Faloney was good on 14 of 20 for 272 yards. Along the ground, Ticats gained 172 yards and the Lions only 93. Lions penetrated Hamilton territory only five times—once in the second quarter and only twice in each of the third and fourth quarters.

Two of Hamilton's touchdowns came on passes—a seven-yarder to Willie Bethea in the second quarter and an electrifying 70-yard pass-and-run touchdown by veteran Hal Patterson in the third. Art Baker scored the other on a one-yard plunge in the second. Don Sutherin kicked the converts.

Peter Kempf kicked a 29-yard field goal for Lions in the second period and the Lions polished off an 81-yard march in six plays in the final minutes of the game when Kapp shot a five-yarder to Mac Burton in the Tiger-Cat end zone. Kempf converted.

Patterson's touchdown was his fifth—and last—in Cup play, a record. And the six points brought his Cup total to 28, just two short of the all-time mark of 30 set by Joe Krol with Hamilton Flying Wildcats and Toronto Argonauts in the 1940s and early 1950s.

The Lions vowed they would roar in 1964, and they weren't talking. Argonauts said wait until 1964, and they were whistling. They improved, though. From a three-win 1963 season, they made it four in 1964, dropped back to three in 1965, and Jackie Parker fled.

CHAPTER XXX

JOE KAPP TO VICTORY

Nov. 28, 1964, at Toronto
British Columbia Lions 34, Hamilton Tiger-Cats 24

A peanut butter pusher, a third-string fullback and a poetry-writing second-string quarterback combined to honor a promise Lions had made to their fans.

It was a little late, mind you—11 years to be precise—but the Lions dug up their club-birth slogan "Lions Roar in '54" and updated it with a 1964 Grey Cup victory. Until this season, and with only a few exceptions, they had been able to emit nothing much more dangerous than a yelp in the Western Conference.

Joe Kapp, the peanut butter man, Bill Munsey, the fullback who had carried the ball only once for no gain in two years of professional football, and Pete Ohler the poet were the main architects of Lions' smashing victory over Tiger-Cats, the powerhouse of the East. No one figured that the comparative unknowns—Muncey and Ohler—would play a prominent part in the victory but between them they were responsible for three of the five B.C. touchdowns.

Kapp, the rangy Californian and leader of the Lions' drive to their two-straight Western Conference first-place finishes and a spot in the East-West final, was a natural, the acknowledged leader. And his name was worth money to promotion-minded companies with a product to sell. He had a company aptly named Joe Kapp, Ltd., that promoted automobiles and, in the past, pushed a hair dressing purporting to be the antithesis of "greasy kid stuff."

Peanut butter, though, was his big off-season deal. "He sure sells a lot of peanut butter for us," said one executive of the bread spread company. Joe toured the B.C. countryside in a peanut butter-colored convertible, made more than 100 personal appearances.

Muncey, who got no farther than the line of scrimmage in his one ball-carrying effort in a Western Conference game in 1963, scored two touchdowns in three minutes and four seconds in the third quarter. They couldn't have come at a more opportune time. Tiger-Cats sniffing blood and on the prowl, had cut the Lions' lead to 20-8 when Muncey went to work. Playing in the fullback slot left vacant by a knee injury to first-string Bob Swift and a leg ailment to second-stringer Neal Beaumont, he rambled 18 yards for his first TD.

On the last play of the quarter and with Ticats on the B.C. 35, Johnny Counts fumbled a long lateral from Bernie Faloney. Dick Fouts, B.C. defensive end, booted the loose ball, Muncey was there to grab it on the run and he streaked 65 yards for the touchdown that ended the Lions' scoring.

The scoreboard showed Lions in front 34-8. Ticats were dead and every one in the crowd of 32,655 at the Canadian National Exhibition Stadium knew it, although a desperation last-quarter rally netted them 16 points on two converted touchdowns and a conceded safety touch. Ohler's contribution came on a broken play early in the second quarter with Lions in front 7-0.

B.C. lined up for a field goal attempt from the Hamilton 19. Ohler fumbled the punt, retrieved the ball and pitched an end zone pass to Jim Carphin, a second-string end who had been detailed to act as an emergency receiver in the event of any miscues on the snap. Coach Dave Skrien of the Lions said it was "definitely" a broken play. The 23-year-old Ohler said he had been practising the pass to Carphin for just such an eventuality.

Lions' other touchdowns came from Swift on a one-yard hurdle over the line and a 46-yard dash around end by incomparable Willie Fleming who was a terror all afternoon. Peter Kempf clicked on four of five convert attempts and Beaumont conceded the two-point safety.

Counts scored one Hamilton touchdown on a 56-yard sideline ramble after taking a lateral from Faloney in the third quarter and Faloney tossed touchdown strikes to Tommy Grant and Stan Crisson in the final 15 minutes when the game was out of reach.

Don Sutherin converted two touchdowns and Joe Zuger kicked two singles. The statistics didn't prove a thing in this one, except possibly to show that figures can lie. Tiger-Cats gained 203 yards on the ground against 150 for Lions. They outpassed them 233-159. They ran up 22 first downs against 16 for B.C. Kapp kept the supposedly-tough Hamilton defence off balance most of the afternoon. He picked holes in Hamilton's deep pass defence. He crossed up the big, tough front wall by sending 183-pound Fleming down the middle instead of steering him out wide.

And Tiger-Cats couldn't do much about it. Fleming, who went out of the 1963 Cup final with a mild concussion, barrelled through the Hamilton line for 67 yards on six rushes and caught two passes for 36 yards. It was British Columbia's last appearance in the Cup final before football rounded the corner into the 1970s. But two East-West appearances in 11 years was good for a club that had to start from scratch. The Western Conference refused player help in any way and B.C. was faced with the job of building a nucleus of Canadian talent on his own in 1954.

Operation of the club also was a big problem. At one time Lions had 3,500 club members who had a hand in decision-making. Each had contributed $20 to the team and they all had something to say about the operation. Finally, an investigation in 1960 sparked by a Vancouver barber, got to the heart of the matter and succeeded in streamlining the executive down from 30 men to nine and cut away the powers of the 3,500 club members.

The club also went through four coaches starting with Annis Stukus in 1954 before it could make it to the Cup final in 1963. It was a great roar the Lions let out in 1964. But consider the plight of Winnipeg Blue Bombers. They had taken an unexpected tumble into fourth place in the West in 1963 and missed the playoffs for the first time since 1949. This year was a disaster. They won only one game, tied another and suffered 14 losses—13 of them in a row.

Their trainer, Gordie Mackie, could justifiably claim that he had more television exposure than any football trainer in the country. He didn't intend it that way, but he was pushed into the limelight by the Bombers. Mackie spent much of his time during Bomber games dashing out onto the field in aid of fallen players. No fewer than 20 suffered serious injuries on the field during the season.

"I had a lot of TV time," said Mackie who was named to coach Canada's 1954 British Empire Games boxing team, but who couldn't make the trip to Vancouver because of other commitments. The 1964 game marked the end of Cup play for Bernie Faloney and his two touchdown passes added to his previous total set a Cup record of eight, matched only by Russ Jackson of Ottawa Rough Riders in 1969.

CHAPTER XXXI

THE SAFETY-TOUCH DEBACLE

Nov. 27, 1965, at Toronto
Hamilton Tiger-Cats 22, Winnipeg Blue Bombers 16

Since taking over Winnipeg Blue Bombers in 1957, Coach Bud Grant had gone along with the theory that sound, basic football with a few wrinkles added here and there would pay off. It did, until this Grey Cup day.

In the 1958 Cup final he drove Tiger-Cats wild with a seldom-seen play, a pitchout to the halfback who followed with a forward pass to the quarter who had scooted downfield. He crossed up Ticats with the quick kick a year later and won each time.

This time, though, was different because of conditions never seen before in the East-West final: winds of 30 to 40 miles an hour that gusted up to 50 miles an hour in the waterfront Canadian National Exhibition stadium. Game plans gone with the big blow, Bombers conceded three safety touches, six points, and then lost by this heartbreaking margin. If anything, the lesson learned was that you never make voluntary contributions to the Tiger-Cat cause.

Why did he do it? Grant's reasoning was sound. "It is better to give up six points than 21," he said. What he meant, of course, was that if Bombers had punted against the wind the Tiger-Cats would be in good field position for touchdowns.

Each time the Bombers conceded the safety touch they had possession of the ball inside their own 25-yard line. The thing to do was to take the third-down snap, scramble back into the Bomber end zone, give up two points but retain possession of the ball with first down on its own 25-yard line.

"We knew that all three safeties were calculated risks," Grant said. "But we could not let them have the ball by punting against that wind.'

His players backed him up. And the 36,655 fans at the game and the millions of television viewers would go along with the concessions because long before half-time they had given up trying to figure out just what was going on out there. They weren't alone. Many of the players on the field and knowledgeable football men in the stands were just as perplexed.

General manager Lew Hayman of Toronto Argonauts was one. He had been closely associated with football as coach and club official for more than 30 years and the only conclusion he could reach was that the rule on punts had been altered. "My feeling is that if certain conditions necessitate a change, it should be announced over the public address system to advise the people," he said.

Jake Gaudaur, president of Hamilton Tiger-Cats, was another. He grabbed Ticat Coach Ralph Sazio immediately after the game to ask for an explanation of what he thought was "strange officiating." He wanted to know just what was going on and Jake had been a player and official for more than 25 years. If these men were perplexed, you can only hazard a guess as to the state of mind of the paying spectators and TV viewers. But the rule on punts in such a situation as this one hadn't been altered.

One play in the third quarter had John Barrow, nine-year Ticat linebacker and tackle, talking to himself. Bomber punter Ed Ulmer kicked from the Winnipeg 25-yard line. The wind blew the ball back to him and Barrow, standing right there, stole the ball from Ulmer's hand and ran for a touchdown. It didn't count. Officials gave Hamilton possession.

"The officials really gave with the razzle-dazzle on that play," Barrow said after the game. "One claimed the punt had not gone over the line of scrimmage. Another said 'no yards.' "I wasn't sure of my ground so I backed off."

Here is the rule in the books: "Should the ball on a kick from scrimmage travel only a short distance across the line of scrimmage and the players of the kicker's team have had no opportunity to give the receiving player the necessary yards the referee may, immediately the ball touches a player or the ground, declare the ball dead, and the ball shall go to the receiving team, but there shall be no penalty assessed for failure to give yards."

Game officials went to great pains before the game to acquaint—or refresh the memories—of the team coaches about it.

That was the thing to do under the unusual playing conditions. The coaches and players at least would have some idea what to expect on punts against the high winds. And the Canadian Football League pulled a blunder. It didn't bother to tell the people who paid up to $12 a seat about the rule in force, and fans aren't accustomed to going to games with rule books clutched in hot hands.

The game itself was something of a thriller, although it was almost impossible to pass against the strong winds and it was dangerous to punt with the wind in your face as the statistics showed. Joe Zuger of Ticats had an average of 29 yards on six punts against the wind and Ulmer averaged only 17 yards on eight boots, also against the wind.

All points, excluding the safeties, were scored by the team with the wind at its back. Tiger-Cats went ahead 10-0 in the first quarter, fell behind 13-10 in the second and took a 22-13 lead into the final period when Bombers could manage only a field goal by Norm Winton. In this quarter, too, the Tiger-Cat defensive unit made Bombers yield possession on two of three third-down gambles.

Art Perkins and Leo Lewis scored the Bomber touchdowns on eight- and five-yard gallops and Winton added one convert and his 14-yard last-quarter field goal. Besides the six gift points, Tiger-Cats counted two converted touchdowns and two singles. Dick Cohee skirted seven yards around end for the first touchdown in the opening quarter and Willie Bethea combined with Zuger for a 69-yard pass-and-run touchdown in the third. Don Sutherin kicked the converts and a single on the game's opening kickoff when Dave Raimey was downed in the Winnipeg end zone.

Grant, seeking his fifth victory against Ticats in their sixth clash since 1957, conceded his first safety in the opening quarter and gave up the others in the third session. It was his last appearance in the Cup.

And it was the second—and last—Cup victory for Sazio as coach. He made his head-coaching debut in 1963 with a 21-10 decision over British Columbia Lions and in 1968 he moved up as general manager when Jake Gaudaur took over as CFL commissioner. And the CFL decided in 1970 to do something about conceded safety touches in order to retain possession of the ball. Under the new rule the defending team is allowed the option of declining to accept the two points. The defending team now "can elect to have the play ruled as an ordinary incompleted pass," with the team in possession going ahead with the next play from the previous line of scrimmage. That is okay with Ralph Sazio who said of the conceded safeties after the 1965 contest: "Did I ever concede a point in any game?"

CHAPTER XXXII

RON LANCASTER DAY

Nov. 26, 1966, at Vancouver
Saskatchewan Roughriders 29, Ottawa Rough Riders 14

Al Ritchie missed fulfilment of his dreams by nine months. He died Feb. 22, 1966. For more than 40 years he had looked forward to the day when Saskatchewan Roughriders would win the Grey Cup. Eight times the Roughriders had travelled East in search of the trophy and eight times they had lost.

It turned out he was the only coach to lose four straight in the national final. That happened from 1929 through 1932 and, although frustrating and disappointing, it really didn't matter that much. Those setbacks were to be expected at a time when the West, pitifully short of Canadian-born players compared with the player-rich East, was trying to keep the game alive on a national scale. Ironic, too, was the fact that Roughriders lost money on their pilgrimages East in these depression years.

Ritchie had twice come close when Regina, as the team then was known, lost 14-3 to the Tigers at Hamilton in 1929 and 11-6 to Balmy Beach at Toronto in 1930. Roughriders had played in almost intolerable weather and field conditions. They were ridiculed by Eastern critics and their appeal at the game was something less than sensational.

Only twice in Ritchie's era did Roughriders attract more than 5,000 spectators at a Cup final in the East—8,629 at Kingston in 1923 when they were beaten 54-0 by Queen's University and 5,112 at Montreal in 1931 when they were shut out 22-0 by the Winged Wheelers. But Al Ritchie knew that some day the Roughriders would bust through to win.

That day could have come exactly 30 years ago, in 1936, but Regina became tangled up in Canadian Rugby Union red tape and was booted out of the East-West final. That year Roughriders defeated Winnipeg

Blue Bombers, defending Cup champions, 24-12 in the two-game total-point Western semi-final and Calgary 3-1 in the sudden-death final.

Unknown to them, that 3-1 victory was their finale for the year. The CRU ruled that they had five Americans on the roster who didn't qualify for Cup final play under newly-instituted regulations declaring imports must be resident in Canada before Jan. 1, 1936. Instead, the ORFU champion Sarnia Imperials met Ottawa Rough Riders in the all-Eastern final.

Ritchie went back to his job as scout for New York Rangers of the National Hockey League and he was out of the picture 15 years later, in 1951, when Saskatchewan next made it to the Cup final, and lost 21-14 to Ottawa.

In 1966, again after a 15-year wait, the Roughriders went all the way. Amid the jubilation in Regina, it is reasonable to assume that a few sentimental football fans turned thoughts to the man whose perseverance against long odds many years ago deserved a spot with others who helped make the East-West classic the No. 1 sports attraction in the country.

The citizens of Regina had honored him once before. He had coached Regina Pats to the 1928 Canadian junior football title, the first time the West had won it, and in 1930 citizens presented him with a car and a plaque.

That was a highlight in the career of Ritchie, born in Cobden, Ont., Dec. 12, 1896, and who had gone west as a young man. But this 1966 Cup victory probably would have been more satisfying. The Roughriders, formed in 1910 and the oldest football team in Western Canada, went into the final with the dubious distinction of being the only team in the nine-club Canadian Football League never to win the trophy. They erased this with an ease that stunned the Easterners and 36,553 fans at Empire Stadium.

Ron Lancaster, the quarterback who started the 1960 Cup final for Ottawa and was replaced early in that game by Russ Jackson, proved that on this day at least he was the finest passer in the country. A Cup record five touchdown passes were thrown and Lancaster clicked on three of them to Jim Worden, Al Ford and Hugh Campbell. Jackson tossed a pair to Whit Tucker. George Reed of Saskatchewan scored the only touchdown along the conventional ground route, a 31-yard burst down the middle in the final quarter.

Ottawa started with a flourish that threatened to chase the Western club right back to Regina. Rough Riders piled up eight first downs in the opening 15 minutes during which the jittery Western Riders jumped offside four times.

Regina settled down after the change of ends and allowed Ottawa to move the yardsticks another four times, mainly in the second quarter when Tucker latched on to his second TD pass. Saskatchewan defenders dug in and did not allow Ottawa to penetrate the Western end of the field in the last half.

At times, the action in the stands was more spirited than the play. And for the second time in seven years at Empire Stadium, the Cup final was halted by unruly mobs. In 1960, the Edmonton-Ottawa contest was called with 41 seconds remaining when thousands of persons invaded the field. This time, spectators raced onto the field and milled around the players with four seconds showing on the clock. This was mild stuff compared with the downtown street rioting the eve of the game after the Cup parade.

More than 5,000 law-abiding citizens flocked downtown for an inexpensive night out on the town, and when the parade ended the hoodlums took over. The police haul was 689 persons in four hours of rioting. They broke store windows, ripped street decorations, lit fires in ornamental trash cans, indulged in a wild bottle-throwing melee, engaged in beer bottle attacks. When order was restored the count was 159 charged with unlawful assembly, another 115 were in jail charged with drunkenness and malicious damage and hundreds others were booked on a variety of counts.

Police were still sorting out the charges nearly 60 hours after the game and courts were choked with cases for days. Civic authorities said the hoodlum element used the celebration as an excuse for lawlessness. "If you doubt that," said City Prosecutor Stewart McMorran, "consider the case of the man who had given his girl friend bail money before he left home for the downtown area."

The Grey Cup record book and Vancouver's police blotter were companion documents in the history of the East-West classic. It had reached the point in the 1960s when some reporters kept two sets of statistics—one on the game itself and the other on the number of persons nabbed by police while conducting their own concrete jungle games on downtown streets.

In 1963, for instance, the haul was 319 and The Canadian Press carried the statistics much along the lines of its game statistics showing the first downs, passes tried and complete, and so on. It went like this:

Intoxication	249	Damaging property	6
Fighting	15	Impaired driving	13
Unlawful assembly	28	Reckless driving	1
Obstructing police	3	Drunken driving	1
Assault	3	Total	319

CHAPTER XXXIII

THE KEITH DAVEY EPISODE

Dec. 2, 1967, at Ottawa
Hamilton Tiger-Cats 24, Saskatchewan Roughriders 1

Some politicians don't fade away. They simply swallow themselves one foot at a time. So it was with Keith Davey. The one-time boy wonder of federal Liberal party politics showed considerable agility by vaulting from a seat in the red-carpeted Senate chamber at Ottawa to the post of Canadian Football League commissioner in Toronto.

The marriage lasted only 54 days when the 40-year-old Senator landed on his mod-garbed bottom before he really had time to warm the swivel chair at CFL headquarters. The Davey saga started on June 22, 1966, when the CFL signed him to a three-year $25,000-a-year contract as commissioner with one important escape clause: Either side could terminate the contract after six months.

He would take over on Jan. 1, 1967, from the retiring G. Sydney Halter, the Winnipeg bachelor lawyer who had ruled the CFL since Jan. 17, 1958. "I believe it is important to the Senate that I do a good job as commissioner and it is important to the league that I do a good job as a Senator," Davey said on his appointment. Well spoken, chorused football officials and fellow Senators. And it would have been fine if he had stopped talking right there, but the ebullient Senator was just warming up. He had everyone in the palm of his hands at that point, but somehow those feet of his got in the way.

He had done a great job as national Liberal party organizer and as the key architect of the party's surge to power in the Commons in the 1963 general election. He resigned from the party job after the 1965 election when the Liberals failed to achieve the Commons majority they expected. As a reward for his efforts, Prime Minister Lester Pearson appointed the one-time Toronto radio station sales manager to a seat in the Senate.

Some CFL officials were impressed by his credentials although the unanimous choice as Halter's successor was Jake Gaudaur, president of Hamilton Tiger-Cats and certainly one of the most knowledgeable football men in the country. But Jake wasn't available. The CFL finally settled on the Senator. In a well-publicized interview with sports columnist Dick Beddoes of the Toronto Globe and Mail, Dec. 2, 1967, Davey was up to his sideburns in hot water. He told Beddoes that the CFL needed more consistency in its officiating East and West. He questioned the propriety of having the CFL's top football awards—outstanding player, lineman, Canadian—sponsored by a distillery. He looked back to the hundreds of arrests in weekend rioting during the 1966 Grey Cup "festivities" at Vancouver and said something must be done to "tone up" the East-West final.

He recalled the low scores during the 1965 season and advocated wrapping up defensive football with the garbage. He made a few other pertinent statements that gave football officials' a malady known as a slow burn. The Senator may have been right and the pertinent statements he made probably should have been said—but behind closed doors at CFL sessions.

He had not learned one obvious fact of life: When you are in the entertainment business—as football is—don't knock the product publicly. He told a service luncheon he would resign as commissioner if he found he was expected to become a rubber stamp for league directors. Every football man in the country knew then that Davey had talked himself out of a job. The confrontation took place in Montreal on Feb. 23, 1967, when Davey submitted his report to the CFL.

He asked for a vote of confidence. Toronto Argonauts moved that the CFL give him this. There wasn't a seconder. The commissioner then said he was resigning and there was an unanimous vote, including one from Argonauts, to accept the resignation. Davey stormed out of the meeting and Lew Hayman, president of Argonauts, moved that the CFL pay Davey six months' salary—$12,500. Again, there was no seconder.

Meanwhile, the Senator met reporters waiting outside the CFL meeting room and said: ". . . I believe that most Canadian football fans are thoroughly familiar with the issues here today. They know what I stand for and what I stand against. . . . The owners and I are miles apart in our approach to Canadian professional football. In the circumstances, I have no choice but to submit my resignation as commissioner. . . ."

170

The next day, Feb. 24, Allan McEachern of British Columbia Lions and the incoming president, took over the commissioner's job until April 1, 1968, when Jake Gaudaur, the man the CFL wanted in the first place, took over. What would the CFL do with Senator Davey's report? "Well," said McEachern with a mischievous twinkle in his eye, "put it in the Hall of Fame, I guess."

There will be no such light-hearted frivolity when it comes time to elect Jacob Gill Gaudaur to the Hall. Football has been his life since 1941, except for a four-year stint as an RCAF pilot in the Second World War. He knew it as a six-foot-two 245-pound centre with Toronto Argonauts that year, Toronto RCAF-Hurricanes as 1942 Grey Cup champions, Toronto Indians of the Ontario Rugby Football Union in 1946, Hamilton Tiger-Cats of the Big Four from 1950 until 1953 when Ticats won the Cup with a 12-6 victory over Winnipeg Blue Bombers.

And he knew it from management side as general manager, president and part owner of Tiger-Cats from 1954 until the eve of his appointment as CFL commissioner, as Big Four president in 1959 and CFL president in 1962. In these years his Tiger-Cats won the Cup four times and had hit the East-West final on nine occasions.

The Davey-CFL war boiled over while the country was warming up to its Centennial celebrations and Ottawa, as the hub of the back-slapping, was getting set to act as host to the 1967 Cup final for the first time since 1940. Ottawa fans hoped the Rough Riders would stuff the Centennial pie by making it against Calgary Stampeders, a big threat in the West and the club, as any fans would recall, that had won an outrageous 12-7 Cup decision over the Riders back in 1948.

And things, indeed, were shaping up this way, thanks to the generosity of the Big Four misfits—Toronto Argonauts and Montreal Alouettes. They had been in the depths of the Big Four standings since the early 1960s and each had been pushing the panic button all this time. This year was no exception. Argos had dropped quarterback Peter Liske, who joined the Stampeders and promptly made the once-proud Eastern club look like a bunch of hacks by winning the outstanding player award in the country. The have-not Als contributed Terry Evanshen to the Calgary cause.

With Liske throwing and Evanshen catching, the Stamps ended the Western schedule in a point tie with Saskatchewan Roughriders, each with 12-4 won-lost records. Roughriders easily disposed of the third-place Edmonton Eskimos 21-5 in the sudden-death semi-final and took on the Stampeders in one of the most spectacular best-of-three Western finals on record.

Stamps won the opener 15-11 at Calgary, were leading 9-8 on a frozen field at Taylor Field in Regina in the second when Evanshen slipped, fell and broke his leg in the third quarter. The Roughies kicked a field goal to win 11-9 and the trip to Ottawa was almost assured. With Evanshen watching from the sidelines, the Stamps lost a 17-13 heart-breaker when Liske's desperation pass in the final minutes was intercepted in the rubber match.

In the East it appeared to be the tired old psychological blackout for Rough Riders in the two-game total-point final with Tiger-Cats. This had been going on since 1963 and, with the exception of 1966, Ticats went on to the final. The Ottawa money called it Rough Riders all the way, particularly after Russ Jackson and company had pushed aside their favorite whipping boys, Toronto Argonauts, 38-22 in the semi-final.

Ticats won a close 11-3 first-game decision and moved into the Cup final with an easy 26-0 victory in the second. Now, for the ninth time since 1957, Ticats were in the East-West classic and they made it look fairly easy against the Roughriders in a game where the only real excitement was provided by over-zealous fans who charged onto the field at various times throughout the game.

Quarterback Joe Zuger scored a touchdown from a couple of yards out, kicked three singles and passed to Ted Watkins, the big pass-catching end who came to an untimely shooting death in California a year later, for another touchdown. Billy Ray Locklin picked up an Ed Buchanan fumble late in the game and ran 43 yards to score and Tommy Joe Coffey scored three points—two on a pair of converts and another on a wide 42-yard field goal attempt.

Saskatchewan's lone point came when Allan Ford quick-kicked from his own 31-yard line. The ball took a series of unpredictable bounces into the Hamilton end zone where Garney Henley was rouged. Overlooked in the post-game celebrations was the fact that Ed Barrow and Tommy Grant had hit the Cup record book. It was their ninth Cup final.

This is a mark unmatched in Cup history. Barrow and Grant each played in the Cup final in 1957-58-59-61-62-63-64-65-67. The 32-year-old Barrow, a graduate from the University of Florida in 1957, was

172

drafted that year by Detroit Lions of the National Football League but joined Tiger-Cats and soon became the acknowledged leader of the defensive corps.

He announced his retirement after the 1969 season but changed his mind in June, 1970. "This is definitely my last year, no kidding," he vowed on June 22, 1970. The six-foot, two-inch defensive tackle and linebacker was named top lineman in the CFL in the 1962 Schenley Award balloting.

Grant, born in Windsor, Ont., was rookie of the year with Tiger-Cats in 1956, and went on to a fine pass-catching career with Ticats until he was traded to Winnipeg Blue Bombers in 1969. He was chosen the outstanding Canadian player in the CFL in the 1954 Schenley voting. From 1956 through 1968, the 32-year-old Grant scored 324 points while with Ticats for an average of 25 points a year.

CHAPTER XXXIV

CALGARY'S JINX

Nov 30, 1968, at Toronto
Ottawa Rough Riders 24, Calgary Stampeders 21

Calgary Stampeders had defeated Saskatchewan Roughriders 32-0 in the opening game of the best-of-three Western Conference final and they acted like losers. The Stamps had been stung too often in the recent past to start talking about a berth in the Cup final.

Four times in the previous five years they had gone into the second game of the Western playoff needing one more victory to advance into the national classic against the Eastern champions. Four times they had lost.

General Manager Rogers Lehew of the Stamps said it for everyone connected with the club this year when he told reporters hours before the second game kickoff that he had no intention of laying in a stock of victory champagne. "When and if we win the West I'll buy the day after the game," he said. There were moments in the second contest when Lehew felt fairly certain that the old playoff jinx was back with the Stampeders and he might not have to buy champagne for at least another year.

Stampeders and Roughriders were tied 10-10 at the end of 60 minutes and many in the crowd at McMahon Stadium in Calgary were about ready to concede that Roughriders could win this one and force a deciding contest, at Taylor Field in Regina. But things started to work for the Stamps in overtime. They won 25-12 and prepared to go east for a meeting with Ottawa Rough Riders.

Many veteran players on the club did not need to jog their memories about their Western Conference playoff frustrations. Since 1962 they had a record of opening-game victories in the final series followed by disastrous second games. One exception was in 1964 when they lost the opener to British Columbia Lions and eventually dropped the series in the three-game limit.

In 1962, Stampeders won the opener 20-14 over Winnipeg Blue Bombers, lost the second 19-11 and dropped the third 12-7 on a final-seconds touchdown by the Bombers.

In 1963 Stampeders started a two-game, total-point semi-final with a 35-9 victory over Saskatchewan, only to have Roughriders perform what is known as the "Little Miracle of Taylor Field" in Regina by winning the return match 39-12 for a 48-47 edge on the round.

Stamps met Winnipeg again in the 1965 and made it look easy with a 27-9 victory in the opener. They lost the second game 15-11, led 8-4 at halftime in the rubber match but two third-quarter touchdowns by Ken Neilsen of the Bombers, one on a play that travelled 109 yards, gave Winnipeg a 19-12 decision and a Cup challenge.

The roof fell in on the Stampeders in the 1967 Western final. They had beaten Saskatchewan 15-11 in the first game of the series, were ahead 9-8 late in the second when Terry Evanshen, their all-star end, suffered a broken leg. Riders went on to win 11-9 and sent Stampeders to the sidelines with a final game 17-13 victory.

But all of this was in the past. Calgary's immediate problem in 1968 was to cart the trophy home for the second time in 20 years. They almost did it. Ottawa had five scoring opportunities in the opening 30 minutes and had scored only four points while the Stamps scored 14 points on touchdowns by quarterback Pete Liske from a yard out and by Evanshen on a 21-yard end zone pass from Liske. Larry Robinson kicked the converts.

The turning point in the game came early in the third quarter when Ron Stewart of Saskatchewan failed to get away a punt and did not make the necessary first-down yardage. Nine plays later Russ Jackson of Ottawa scrambled over from one yard out for a touchdown that cut Calgary's lead to 14-11.

With just 56 seconds of the fourth quarter gone, Vic Washington of the Rough Riders pulled off the play of the game, a 79-yard touchdown run. He had taken a pitchout from Jackson, dropped the ball and it bounced right back into his arms.

With a key block from tackle Tom Benyon, the fast-stepping Ottawa half had a clear road to the Calgary end zone. The convert was blocked, Ottawa led 17-11, and nine minutes later Jackson caught Gene Adkins with a 40-yard pass-and-run touchdown pass. Sutherin converted to end the Ottawa scoring. Sutherin had earlier kicked a single and a 27-yard field goal.

Stampeders made one last desperate attempt in the final minutes of the game after picking up an Ottawa fumble. Evanshen scored on a four-yard pass from Liske, Robinson converted and that was the football game.

Rough Riders had won their second Cup in the 60s but the talk centred around Toronto Argonauts and Leo Cahill, their sophomore coach. Argos had finished second behind Ottawa in the Big Four schedule, polished off the third-place Hamilton Tiger-Cats 33-21 in the sudden-death semi-final and had beaten Ottawa 13-11 in the opener of their two-game total-point Eastern final.

Cahill had put together a hard-hitting collection of players who started talking tough after their first-game playoff victory at Toronto. "Put a Rider and an Argo into a room and the Argo comes out first," one player was quoted as saying. Rough Rider players read this and in the second contest Ottawa clobbered Toronto 36-14 to win the round 47-27.

"All of that tough talk out of Toronto was pretty sickening," Ottawa coach Frank Clair commented. "But it gave us the added incentive to go out and beat them." Rough Riders hadn't heard the last of the Argonaut talk. More was coming up in 1969 and again after Argos had beaten Rough Riders in the opener of the Eastern final.

CHAPTER XXXV

THE RUSS JACKSON SWEEP

Nov. 30, 1969, at Montreal
Ottawa Rough Riders 29, Saskatchewan Roughriders 11

Calgary Stampeder players talked about football shoes. Toronto Argonauts made much to do about walking-around money and an act of God. And Russ Jackson walked on water, said Ottawa Rough Rider fans. Someone stole the Grey Cup and Canadian Football League officials showed remarkable restraint by refusing to panic about it. They knew the trophy would eventually turn up.

The off-the-field action about shoes and money started early in the year, at a time in June when golfers were digging divots, National Hockey League teams were conducting their annual auction of players and the men in football uniforms were trying to sweat off the suet picked up on the banquet circuit.

The Stampeders thought it was time that management should pay the shot for their footwear. Discussions were held, it became a public issue and, almost as fast as the question surfaced, it quietly died out. Everything has been settled, said General Manager Rogers Lehew who declined to say who had won the battle of the cleats. But it was duly noticed that the boys from Canada's oil capital were well shod during the season.

While the Calgary negotiations were being conducted, Argonaut players aired their grievances. It was time, they said, that something was done about expenses during the seven-week training period. They wanted $60 a week for everybody, plus $40 a week retroactive to the start of training for the 32 who made the team.

The talk bounced around for a couple of weeks. One side mentioned "walkout." The other countered with the threat of "suspension" and murmured something about the Canadian Football League's disaster plan whereby players of other teams are recruited to help a club in distress. Finally, on June 19, the players accepted $60 a week for each one attending training camp. Management said it would review the situation for 1970.

These troublesome byplays dispensed with, the CFL settled down to a season highlighted by the showing of Argonauts who at last demonstrated that they belonged with the top clubs in the country. That is, until the playoffs.

They had battled the Grey Cup champion Ottawa Rough Riders down to the wire in three league encounters in the Eastern Conference and had displayed lots of muscle every time out in games East and West. The word soon spread to "get Argos" and the Double Blues, cocky and confident, were willing to take on all comers. They had lost 25-23, 34-27 and 20-9 to Rough Riders in games that could have gone either way.

Finally, they broke through 22-14 in the first contest of the two-game total-point Eastern playoff against Riders and every long-suffering Argo supporter climbed on the bandwagon.

This was the "next year" that fans had ben talking about since 1952 when Argonauts last made it to the Cup final. They couldn't see any way that this edition of the Toronto club could lose to the Riders. Coach Leo Cahill stuck his tongue in his cheek and said he'd go along with that.

"It will take an act of God to beat us," he told the weekly Playback Club luncheon in Toronto a couple of days after the victory. He followed this up with the flat announcement that Argonauts were "physically better than any team in Canada."

Toronto fans said they would drink to that and a few bruised players around the CFL fingered their lumps and were inclined to go along with that last statement. The most prominent were Saskatchewan Roughriders who said they hoped Argos made it to Montreal on Nov. 30 because they had a few personal grudges to settle. Ottawa Rough Riders weren't impressed with the Argonaut talk—or muscles.

On Saturday, Nov. 22, they clobbered Argos 32-3 and 46-25 on the round. It was a romp, nothing much more than a tough scrimmage. They hammered Argos hard and often and supporters of the red, black and white-shirted Riders weren't a bit bashful about stuffing Cahill's words down his thoat. Some irreverent souls said that Jackson didn't bother to ride to Lansdowne Park, site of the slaughter. He simply walked across the ice floes of the Rideau Canal to get there, they said.

Others playfully clucked that Cahill could have put the Twelve

Apostles in Argo double blue uniforms this cold afternoon and Jackson and his cohorts would have whipped them on the scoreboard and physically. It was a long, torturous afternoon for Argos whose defence was shattered and whose offence sputtered and died.

Riders carried their momentum right into the Autostade in Montreal a week later for Jackson's farewell to football after 12 great years during which he quarterbacked Frank Clair-coached clubs to three Cup titles starting in 1960. And this year he had personally won every award and honor worth winning.

A crowd of 33,172 looked on as Jackson proved he was every bit as much a money player as another Canadian-born great, Joe Krol of Argonauts who rose to the heights in the post-war years when he led Argos to three straight Cup titles over Winnipeg Blue Bombers. Jackson had to go out a winner and he accomplished it with brisk efficiency. Going right along with him was his backfield sidekick, little Ron Stewart, another 12-year man who played a fantastic game.

Saskatchewan Roughrider linemen and linebackers got close enough to peer down Jackson's throat on many occasions but the 32-year-old native of Hamilton, Ont. squirmed, ducked, back-pedalled, fled for his own well-being and somehow managed to hit targets with his aerial bombs, side-armed or by the conventional overhand route. It didn't seem to matter.

The Western champions made it known early that their Eastern counterparts would have a rough day. They piled up a 9-0 first-quarter lead on a touchdown by Alan Ford, converted by Jack Abendschan, and a two-point safety touch concession by Ottawa.

The TD was set up when Bill Van Burkleo slipped while attempting to punt. Ken Reed recovered for Saskatchewan and quarter Ron Lancaster threw a perfect strike to Ford who went over the Ottawa line. Ottawa didn't get into Saskatchewan territory until the final sequence of plays in the opening quarter. From that point on Jackson got his offensive unit clicking and the Rough Rider defence dug in when the wheat province club's downfield marches penetrated deep into the Ottawa end of the field.

Jackson threw four touchdown passes—a Cup record. That brought his total in four East-West championship games to a record-equalling eight established by Bernie Faloney of Hamilton Tiger-Cats. Jackson clicked on TD passes to Jay Roberts and Jim Mankins and a pair to Stewart, who played one of the finest games of his brilliant career.

179

Stewie, a little five-foot-seven 175-pounder and rated one of the deadliest blocking backs in Canadian football throughout the 1960s, left Saskatchewan players clawing on the ground as he burst through for touchdowns of 80 and 32 yards.

Stewart's performance was reminiscent of his finest hour in a league game against Montreal Alouettes on Oct. 11, 1960. In that one he carried the ball 15 times, scored four touchdowns and piled up a remarkable 287 yards, a Canadian single-game record.

That same year Stewart and Jackson were the pick of the Riders when they beat Edmonton Eskimos 16-6 in the Cup final at Vancouver. And here, nine years later, they were the one-two punch that again broke the West's heart. The press box inhabitants named Jackson the outstanding player of the game with 103 votes against 93 for runner-up Stewart. Jackson won a new car. Stewart was presented by fellow-players with the game ball.

There were more honors coming for Jackson who already had won the Schenley Award as the outstanding football player in the country and had been chosen for the Eastern Conference and all-Canada all-star teams.

On Dec. 19, he was one of 22 Canadians who received the medal of service of the Order of Canada. Selections made are for "merit, especially service to Canada and humanity at large." Later on, he was voted the outstanding athlete of Canada in the annual CP year-end poll and in another CP poll was named most newsworthy Canadian outside public affairs.

Not bad for a man who played for McMaster University in Hamilton and who turned down a Rhodes scholarship in 1957 to play pro football with Riders. Toronto-born Stewart, who also joined Riders in 1957, proved throughout his career that he also could rate among the finest Canadian-born stars.

Lost in the fuss over Jackson and Stewart and the fine overall play of the Rough Riders were a couple of fellows whose accomplishments merited conspicuous note. Don Sutherin, Ottawa's defensive half, moved into the Cup's Big Ten scoring list—the only active player in the CFL to make it into this exclusive club dating back to 1909—with a five-point afternoon on four converts and a single. This brought his Cup total to 23, just seven behind all-time top scorer Joe Krol of Toronto Argonaut fame.

The other belonged to Frank Clair. The victory marked the fifth time he had coached a Cup winner, matching the record set by Lew Hayman. Clair, who moved upstairs as general manager of the club 10 days after the Cup final, had coached Toronto Argonauts to the championship in 1950 and 1952 and Rough Riders in 1960, 1968 and 1969. Hayman had winners with Toronto Argonauts in 1933, 1937 and 1938, Toronto RCAF-Hurricanes in 1942 and Montreal Als in 1949.

Clair moved into the spot vacated by Red O'Quinn who quit to take the same job with Montreal. And one of the first official duties of O'Quinn, great pass-catching end with the Als in the 1950s, was to sign as head coach the man who threw him the passes in those days—Sam Etcheverry. Jack Gotta, assistant to Clair for two years, was appointed head coach of the Riders. And 1970 started as a great year for the CFL.

Gross gate receipts from the 1969 game were $405,000 — the first $400,000 gate in Canadian football history. The Grey Cup, stolen Dec. 20, 1969, from Lansdowne Park, was picked up by police on Feb. 16, 1970, in a locker in the Royal York Hotel in Toronto. And almost three weeks later—on March 3—the CFL hit the jackpot.

The Canadian Radio-Television Commission announced a ban on the importation of CFL games by cable television operators in areas where local TV stations are blacked out. A dispute had been going on for several years between the CFL and the cable companies over the circumvention of home-game blackouts.

Cable TV had cut into attendance at some parks, particularly in Ottawa where Rider officials blamed it for a sharp decline in attendance in 1969, an average loss of about 4,000 spectators a game at Lansdowne Park. The CRTC ban, too, put the CFL on solid footing in negotiations with advertisers for game rights.

CFL Commissioner Jake Gaudaur was enthusiastic about the CRTC ruling. "We've always been sympathetic to the point of view of the cable systems, but . . . the home blackout is essential to our survival," he said. "Surely this is the only instance where somebody can take a commodity produced by somebody else, sell it and also contribute to the eventual destruction of the original producer."

The CFL had its trophy back and the CRTC ruling iced the cake. Everything was right with the Canadian pro football world, but not for long. In June, 1970, reports circulated that the Canadian Football League Players' Association would call a strike over the still-unsettled training camp salary question immediately following the July 2 game at Ottawa between the CFL All-Stars and the defending Cup champion Rough Riders. These reports, denied by Mike Wadsworth of Toronto Argonauts, Players' Association president, persisted until late afternoon of the all-star game.

Three hours before the kickoff Gaudaur announced, following a meeting with John Agro of Hamilton, executive director of the Players' Association, that agreement had been reached. Neither would give details of the agreement. "We are extremely pleased with the end result," Agro said.

The all-star game was played before a crowd of 23,094, including 21-year-old Prince Charles who had arrived in Canada just a few hours before. All-Stars won 35-14 and the prince presented the Canada Permanent Trust Trophy to Greg Findlay of British Columbia Lions, captain of the All-Stars, and also a special trophy to quarterback Ron Lancaster of Saskatchewan Roughriders, voted the game's outstanding player by reporters.

Jackson came out of retirement for this game only. He completed three of eight passes for 28 yards and had two passes intercepted. His last pass, probably his final in football, was intercepted in the final seconds of the game.

The Grey Cup

Statistical Record

1909-1970

GREY CUP MILESTONES

1909: Governor-General Earl Grey offers Cup for "amateur rugby in Canada."

Dec. 4, 1909: University of Toronto first winner, defeats Toronto Parkdale 26-6; Hughie Gall of Varsity kicks Cup record eight singles; ticket prices $1.25, 50 cents and 25 cents.

Nov. 26, 1910: University of Toronto defeats Hamilton Tigers 16-7 at Hamilton; ticketless fans break down fences, 2,000 get in free.

Nov. 25, 1911: University of Toronto defeats Toronto Argonauts 14-7, third straight Cup victory for college champions.

Dec. 3, 1921: Edmonton Eskimos first West challengers, lose 23-0 to Toronto Argonauts at Toronto; teams cut to 12 players from 14.

Dec. 1, 1923: Queen's University defeats Regina Roughriders 54-0, record one-team score; Queen's score record one-game nine touchdowns; Pep Leadlay kicks record seven converts.

Nov. 29, 1924: Queen's defeats Toronto Balmy Beach 11-3, second team to win three straight; no East-West game for first of six times (1924-26-27, 1936, 1940, 1944); officials and players of Winnipeg Victorias squabble over railway line to be used for transportation East, differences settled but too late to challenge Queen's.

Dec. 5, 1925: Ottawa Senators defeat Winnipeg Tammany Tigers 24-1 at Ottawa; sports writers say "something must be done to stop these East-West fiascos."

Dec. 1, 1928: Grey Cup broadcast for first time; Hamilton Tigers defeat Regina Roughriders 30-0 at Hamilton.

Nov. 30, 1929: Forward passes thrown for first time in a Cup final; passes could not be tossed from within 25 yards of the opposition's goal line; Hamilton Tigers defeat Regina Roughriders 14-3.

Dec. 6, 1930: Canadian Rugby Union schedules Cup-day doubleheader; Toronto Balmy Beach defeats Regina Roughriders 11-6 in Cup; Toronto Argonauts defeat Winnipeg Native Sons 7-4 in Canadian junior championship opener.

Feb. 28, 1931: CRU adopts forward pass, rules it may not be thrown from inside defensive team's 25-yard line.

Dec. 5, 1931: First Cup touchdown pass—Warren Stevens to Kenny Grant in Montreal Winged Wheelers' 22-0 win over Regina Roughriders; Red Tellier of Montreal banished from football for life for attack on George Gilhooley, Regina player, after game; Tellier reinstated three years later.

Dec. 2, 1933: Winnipegs lose 13-0 to Toronto Argonauts in Cup semi-final at Toronto—first, and last time Western champions forced to play sudden-death semi-final in the East.

Dec. 9, 1933: Toronto Argonauts defeat Sarnia Imperials 4-3 for Cup.

Nov. 24, 1934: Alex Hayes of Sarnia Imperials drop-kicks two converts and a field goal as Imps beat Regina Roughriders 20-12 at Toronto, the last display of drop-kicking in a Cup final.

Dec. 7, 1935: West wins first Cup; Winnipegs defeat Hamilton Tigers 18-12 at Hamilton; Winnipegs' Fritzie Hanson runs wild.

Dec. 5, 1936: Sarnia Imperials defeat Ottawa Rough Riders 26-20 at Toronto; CRU rules Regina Roughriders ineligible to play in final because they did not adhere to newly-adopted regulations saying only American residents of Canada before Jan. 1 were eligible to play during regular schedule.

1937: Intercollegiate Union withdraws from Cup competition.

Dec. 10, 1938: Toronto Argonauts defeat Winnipeg Blue Bombers 30-7; Red Storey gets off bench in final quarter to score three touchdowns and set up another.

Dec. 9, 1939: Last-second single by Art Stevenson gives Winnipeg Blue Bombers 8-7 win over Ottawa Rough Riders at Ottawa.

Nov. 23, 1940: CRU rules Winnipeg Blue Bombers, Western champions, not eligible for Cup play due to playing-rules dispute.

Nov. 30, 1940: Ottawa Rough Riders defeat Toronto Balmy Beach 8-2 at Toronto in first game of only two-game total-point Cup final in history.

Dec. 7, 1940: Ottawa defeats Beaches 12-5 to take round 20-7 at Ottawa; 1,700 fans is smallest crowd in Cup history, gate receipts of $1,798 also smallest.

Dec. 13, 1940: West pulls out of CRU.

Dec. 15, 1940: James Bannerman of Calgary, CRU president, resigns.

Feb. 22, 1941: West returns to CRU.

Nov. 29, 1941: Cup record five field goals kicked as Winnipeg Blue Bombers defeat Ottawa Rough Riders 18-16 in wild game at Toronto.

Dec. 5, 1942: Toronto RCAF-Hurricanes first Armed Forces winner, defeat Winnipeg RCAF-Bombers 8-5.

Dec. 1, 1945: Toronto Argonauts defeat Winnipeg Blue Bombers 35-0 at Toronto, first of three consecutive Cup triumphs for Toronto club.

March 25, 1947: Grey Cup salvaged from fire in Toronto Argonaut Rowing Club blaze.

Nov. 29, 1947: Single by Joe Krol in last seconds gives Toronto Argonauts 10-9 win over Winnipeg Blue Bombers; Argos become third team in Cup history to win three consecutive years; previous three-straight winners: University of Toronto 1909-11, Queen's University 1922-24.

Nov. 27, 1948: Calgary fans make pre-game Cup festival colorful celebration; Stampeders defeat Ottawa Rough Riders 12-7; Calgary scores sleeper-play touchdown, only time in Cup history; tickets $1.50 and $1.

Nov. 26, 1949: Lew Hayman becomes first coach to win five Cup titles as Montreal Alouettes defeat Calgary Stampeders 28-15; Hayman's previous winners—Toronto Argonauts 1933-37-38, Toronto RCAF-Hurricanes 1942. Frank Clair later equals Hayman record with Argonaut teams in 1950-52, Ottawa Rough Riders 1960-68-69.

Nov. 25, 1950: Weather makes "Mud Bowl" game of Toronto Argonaut's 13-0 win over Winnipeg Blue Bombers at Toronto; Jack Wedley of Argos sets record by playing on seven Cup-winning teams, six with Argonauts—1937-38, 1945-46-47-50; one with St. Hyacinthe-Donnacona, 1944.

Oct. 30, 1951: $12,000 tarpaulin, bought by CRU after outraged protests of team and league officials following 1950 Mud Bowl, arrives in Toronto to protect Cup final fields; ticket prices scaled upwards to top of $5.65.

Nov. 24, 1951: Jake Dunlap of Ottawa Rough Riders is first player to be banished from Cup final, thumbed off in fourth quarter for roughing kicker as Ottawa defeats Saskatchewan Roughriders 21-14 at Toronto.

Nov. 29, 1952: Cup final televised first time; Toronto Argonauts defeat Edmonton Eskimos 21-11 at Toronto; Joe Krol of Argos ends brilliant career as highest scorer in Cup history—30 points in seven finals dating to 1943.

March 27, 1953: Interprovincial Union (Big Four) and Western Interprovincial Football Union open door to full control of senior football in Canada and Grey Cup final by gaining voting control of CRU; Big Four and WIFU each received three votes, up from two each; Ontario Rugby Football Union retained its two votes and single votes held by Quebec Rugby Football Union and Eastern Intercollegiate Union.

Nov. 28, 1953: Indian Jack Jacobs of Winnipeg Blue Bombers throws Cup Record 46 passes, none for touchdown; Winnipeg loses 12-6 to Hamilton Tiger-Cats at Toronto; ticket prices raised to $6 top.

Nov. 27, 1954: Edmonton Eskimos score stunning 26-25 victory over 5-to-1 favored Montreal Alouettes at Toronto; Jackie Parker's 85-yard touchdown run in final minutes after picking up fumble by Chuck Hunsinger of Als ties score 25-25; Bob Dean kicks game-winning convert.

March 26, 1955: Vancouver awarded 1955 Cup final, first city in Western Canada to play host to classic; Big Four and WIFU arrange schedules so that time not allowed for an ORFU challenge; new rule says all players in Cup final must wear stockings.

186

Nov. 26, 1955: Crowd of 39,417 at Empire Stadium in Vancouver is largest in Cup play; Sam Etcheverry of Montreal Alouettes sets Cup record 30 pass completions for Cup record 508 yards but ground power gives Edmonton Eskimos 34-19 victory; fans invade end zone on wide Edmonton field goal attempt in fourth quarter, preventing runback and officials award Edmonton a single; tickets scaled up to $7.50, $6, $5 and $4.

Dec. 4, 1955: Big Four and WIFU agree to unite in tentative Canadian Football League; Unions would retain their separate entities as Big Four and WIFU; interlocking Big Four-WIFU schedule okayed.

Jan. 22, 1956: Judge Allan J. Fraser of Ottawa, appointed Big Four commissioner; G. Sydney Halter of Winnipeg, re-appointed WIFU commissioner.

Feb. 10, 1956: Big Four and WIFU organize Canadian Football Council representing the nine teams.

March 26, 1956: Grey Cup prices increased to $10, $7.50, $6 and $5; six-point touchdown adopted.

Nov. 24, 1956: Edmonton Eskimos complete triple over Montreal, win 50-27, fourth team in Cup history to win three straight; others: University of Toronto 1909-11, Queen's University 1922-24; Toronto Argonauts 1945-47; Frank (Pop) Ivy of Eskimos third coach to win three straight—Billy Hughes, Queen's, first with wins in 1922-23-24 and matched by Teddy Morris of Toronto Argonauts in 1945-46-47; fan grabs ball after Edmonton's Jackie Parker scores third touchdown of game with 19 seconds remaining—man with footballs, along with Alouettes, had left the field and convert not attempted as officials signify end of game; scoreboard flashes wrong score—51-27.

Jan. 20, 1957: Canadian Football Council officially votes Ontario Rugby Football Union out of Cup contention; player-position names modernized—stricken from rule books were references to snaps (now centres); inside wings (guards), middle wings (tackles), outside wings (ends).

Nov. 30, 1957: Fan standing on sidelines trips touchdown-bound Ray (Bibbles) Bawel of Hamilton Tiger-Cats, first time spectator interferes with player on field in Cup play; Tiger-Cats go on to score touchdown and defeat crippled Winnipeg Blue Bombers 32-7.

Jan. 17, 1958: Canadian Football League formed, out of picture is Canadian Football Council; G. Sydney Halter of Winnipeg is first CFL commissioner; CFL runs own show on rule changes, import quotas, organization and operation of Cup final.

March 14, 1958: Big Four and Western Conference takes control of CRU—votes of each increased to five from three with ORFU retaining its two votes, Maritimes, Quebec and Intercollegiate unions one each; Big Four-WIFU as such maintains CRU membership.

Nov. 29, 1958: Final returns to Vancouver; Winnipeg Blue Bombers defeat Hamilton Tiger-Cats 35-28; Quarterback Jimmy Van Pelt of Bombers scores one-game record 22 points on two touchdowns, two field goals and four converts; Hamilton's Ralph Goldston ejected from game in second quarter after slugging Winnipeg's Leo Lewis.

Jan. 30, 1959: Canadian Football League adopts constitution; East-West All-Star Shrine game shelved after four years.

Nov. 28, 1959: Winnipeg Blue Bombers score 18 points in final quarter to defeat Hamilton Tiger-Cats 21-7; largest crowd in Eastern Canada football—33,133—see game at Canadian National Exhibition Stadium in Toronto.

Nov. 20, 1960: Canadian Football League agrees to hold partial interlocking East-West schedule.

Nov. 26, 1960: Ottawa Rough Riders defeat Edmonton Eskimos 16-6 in game at Vancouver forced to abrupt and unprecedented halt with 41 seconds remaining as unruly and destructive mob invades playing field; youth steals game ball, makes successful getaway.

Feb. 10, 1961: Canadian Football League approves partial East-West interlocking schedule; starts this year.

187

Feb. 11, 1961: Canadian Football League outlaws sleeper play.

Dec. 2, 1961: Winnipeg Blue Bombers defeat Hamilton Tiger-Cats 21-14 in first overtime Cup game; Blue Bomber quarter Kenny Ploen scores game-winning touchdown at 3:03 of second overtime period in game at Toronto.

Dec. 1-2, 1962: Fog prevents completion of Cup final between Winnipeg Blue Bombers and Hamilton Tiger-Cats with nine minutes and 29 seconds remaining to be played at CNE Stadium in Toronto on Saturday, Dec. 1, and with Bombers ahead 28-27; game resumed at that point on Sunday, Dec. 2, with no further scoring; first time in Cup—and in North American football history—that game played over two-day period.

Nov. 30, 1963: British Columbia Lions make Grey Cup debut, lose 21-10 to Hamilton Tiger-Cats at Vancouver; seat prices scaled up to $12; gate receipts of $341,576.50 and gross revenue of $589,000 largest to date in Cup history.

Nov. 28, 1964: British Columbia Lions win first Grey Cup, beating Hamilton Tiger-Cats 34-24; Pete Ohler fumbles snap on field-goal attempt, passes complete to Jim Carphin on goal line for B.C. touchdown.

Nov. 27, 1965: Winnipeg Blue Bombers concede three safety touches, the margin of victory, as Hamilton Tiger-Cats win Cup 22-16 in high winds at CNE Stadium in Toronto.

June 7, 1966: CRU hands over Grey Cup trophy to CFL as "last gesture"; Union going out of business to be reborn as Canadian Amateur Football Association.

June 22, 1966: CFL appoints Senator Keith Davey as commissioner, succeeding the retiring G. Sydney Halter of Winnipeg; gets three-year $25,000-a-year contract.

Nov. 26, 1966: Saskatchewan Roughriders defeat Ottawa Rough Riders 29-14 in Vancouver for first Cup victory; total of 689 persons arrested in Cup weekend of rioting.

Jan. 1, 1967: Senator Keith Davey takes over as CFL commissioner.

Feb. 23, 1967: Senator Davey resigns as CFL commissioner at meeting in Montreal after 54 days in office.

Dec. 2, 1967: Hamilton Tiger-Cats defeat Saskatchewan Roughriders 24-1 on frozen field at Ottawa; crowd control breaks down, police invade field during game to eject rowdies; ticket prices scaled up to $15; Tommy Grant and John Barrow of Ticats in ninth Cup final, a record.

April 1, 1968: Jake Gaudaur of Hamilton takes over as CFL commissioner.

Nov. 30, 1969: Ottawa Rough Riders defeat Saskatchewan Roughrides 29-11 at Montreal; Ottawa quarterback Russ Jackson throws single-game Cup record four touchdown passes to cap brilliant 12-year pro career; the four TD passes brought his total to eight in Cup play, equalling the record established by Bernie Faloney; Ottawa Coach Frank Clair equals record of coaching five Cup championship teams set by Lew Hayman; players on Cup-winning team receive record $1,500 each, losers $1,000 each; gross gate receipts are $405,000, all-time record; Prime Minister Trudeau makes honorary 28-yard kickoff, also a Cup record.

Dec. 20, 1969: Grey Cup reported stolen from trophy case at Lansdowne Park in Ottawa.

Feb. 16, 1970: Police find Grey Cup in locker in Royal York Hotel, Toronto, after receiving anonymous tip.

GREY CUP'S BIG TEN

DON SUTHERIN, fine defensive halfback and field goal and convert kicker with Hamilton Tiger-Cats and Ottawa Rough Riders, became the only active Canadian Football League player in the exclusive Big Ten scoring race.

He made it Nov. 30, 1969, at Montreal with a five-point afternoon as Ottawa Rough Riders defeated Saskatchewan Roughriders 29-11 to win the Grey Cup for the seventh time in the club's long history.

Sutherin's four converts and one single sent his point-total to 23 in eight Cup finals—six with Tiger-Cats and two with the Rough Riders—and into a six-place Grey Cup Big Ten tie with Pep Leadlay of Queen's University and Hamilton Tiger fame of the 1920s.

Sutherin still is seven points off the pace set by Joe Krol, one of the greatest Canadian-born players the game has seen. Krol, one-time triple threat who had won every known award in Eastern Canada senior football since he joined the University of Western Ontario Mustangs in 1939 and quit football in 1953, scored 30 points in seven Cup appearances.

Krol's points were scored when the touchdown was valued at five points. Three years after his retirement from the game the touchdown value was increased to six.

Here are the Cup's Big Ten (1909-1970):

JOE KROL (30 points)	TD	FG	C	S	Pts
1943 Hamilton Flying Wildcats	0	1	3	1	7
1944 Hamilton Flying Wildcats	0	0	1	0	1
1945 Toronto Argonauts	1	0	2	0	7
1946 Toronto Argonauts	1	0	3	0	8
1947 Toronto Argonauts	0	0	1	4	5
1950 Toronto Argonauts	0	0	0	2	2
1952 Toronto Argonauts	0	0	0	0	0
Totals	2	1	10	7	30
CHARLIE SHEPARD (29)					
1957 Winnipeg Blue Bombers	0	0	0	0	0
1958 Winnipeg Blue Bombers	1	0	0	1	7
1959 Winnipeg Blue Bombers	1	0	0	4	10
1962 Winnipeg Blue Bombers	2	0	0	0	12
Totals	4	0	0	5	29
HAL PATTERSON (28)					
1955 Montreal Alouettes	2	0	0	0	10
1956 Montreal Alouettes	2	0	0	0	12
1961 Hamilton Tiger-Cats	0	0	0	0	0
1962 Hamilton Tiger-Cats	0	0	0	0	0
1963 Hamilton Tiger-Cats	1	0	0	0	6
Totals	5	0	0	0	28
GERRY JAMES (28)					
1953 Winnipeg Blue Bombers	1	0	0	0	5
1957 Winnipeg Blue Bombers	0	0	0	0	0
1958 Winnipeg Blue Bombers	0	0	0	0	0
1959 Winnipeg Blue Bombers	0	1	2	0	5
1961 Winnipeg Blue Bombers	1	2	2	0	14
1962 Winnipeg Blue Bombers	0	0	4	0	4
Totals	2	3	8	0	28

JACKIE PARKER (24)					
1954 Edmonton Eskimos	1	0	0	0	5
1955 Edmonton Eskimos	0	0	0	0	0
1956 Edmonton Eskimos	3	0	0	1	19
1960 Edmonton Eskimos	0	0	0	0	0
Totals	4	0	0	1	24

DON SUTHERIN (23)					
1958 Hamilton Tiger-Cats	0	0	0	0	0
1961 Hamilton Tiger-Cats	0	0	2	0	2
1962 Hamilton Tiger-Cats	0	0	2	1	3
1963 Hamilton Tiger-Cats	0	0	3	0	3
1964 Hamilton Tiger-Cats	0	0	2	0	2
1965 Hamilton Tiger-Cats	0	0	2	1	3
1968 Ottawa Rough Riders	0	1	2	0	5
1969 Ottawa Rough Riders	0	0	4	1	5
Totals	0	1	17	3	23

PEP LEADLAY (23)					
1922 Queen's University	0	0	1	2	3
1923 Queen's University	0	0	7	2	9
1924 Queen's University	0	0	1	3	4
1927 Hamilton Tigers	0	0	0	1	1
1928 Hamilton Tigers	0	0	3	0	3
1929 Hamilton Tigers	0	0	0	3	3
Totals	0	0	12	11	23

JIM VAN PELT (22)					
1958 Winnipeg Blue Bombers	2	2	4	0	22
Totals	2	2	4	0	22

JOHNNY BRIGHT (22)					
1954 Edmonton Eskimos	0	0	0	0	0
1955 Edmonton Eskimos	2	0	0	0	10
1956 Edmonton Eskimos	2	0	0	0	12
1960 Edmonton Eskimos	0	0	0	0	0
Totals	4	0	0	0	22

ROSS CRAIG (21)					
1912 Hamilton Alerts	1	0	1	0	6
1913 Hamilton Tigers	3	0	0	0	15
Totals	4	0	1	0	21

INDIVIDUAL — SINGLE GAME

POINTS SCORED
22 Jim Van Pelt, Winnipeg Blue Bombers, 1958.
19 Jackie Parker, Edmonton Eskimos, 1956.

TOUCHDOWNS
3 Jackie Parker, Edmonton Eskimos, 1956.
Red Storey, Toronto Argonauts, 1938.
Ross Craig, Hamilton Tigers, 1913.

POINTS KICKED
11 George Fraser, Ottawa Rough Riders, 1941.
10 Jim Van Pelt, Winnipeg Blue Bombers, 1958.

FIELD GOALS KICKED
- 3   George Fraser, Ottawa Rough Riders, 1941.
- 2   Gerry James, Winnipeg Blue Bombers, 1961.
  - Steve Oneschuk, Hamilton Tiger-Cats, 1959.
  - Jim Van Pelt, Winnipeg Blue Bombers, 1958.
  - Nick Volpe, Toronto Argonauts, 1950.
  - Ches McCance, Winnipeg Blue Bombers, 1941.
  - Greg Kabat, Winnipeg Blue Bombers, 1938.

CONVERTS KICKED
- 7   Pep Leadlay, Queen's University, 1923.
- 5   Bob Dean, Edmonton Eskimos, 1955.

SINGLES KICKED
- 8   Hughie Gall, University of Toronto, 1909.

BEST PUNTING AVERAGE
52.3 Yards   Bob Isbister, Toronto Argonauts, 1937, (25 punts).

PASSES ATTEMPTED
- 46   Indian Jack Jacobs, Winnipeg Blue Bombers, 1953.

PASSES COMPLETED
- 30   Sam Etcheverry, Montreal Alouettes, 1955.
- 28   Indian Jack Jacobs, Winnipeg Blue Bombers, 1953.

PASSES INCOMPLETE
- 23   Sam Etcheverry, Montreal Alouettes, 1956.

TOUCHDOWN PASSES THROWN
- 4   Russ Jackson, Ottawa Rough Riders, 1969.
- 3   Ron Lancaster, Saskatchewan Rough Riders, 1966.
  - Sam Etcheverry, Montreal Alouettes, 1954.
  - Joe Krol, Toronto Argonauts, 1946.

TOUCHDOWN PASSES CAUGHT
- 2   Ron Stewart, Ottawa Rough Riders, 1969.
  - Terry Evanshen, Calgary Stampeders, 1968.
  - Whit Tucker, Ottawa Rough Riders, 1966.
  - Ron Howell, Hamilton Tiger-Cats, 1958.
  - Hal Patterson, Montreal Alouettes, 1955.
  - Red O'Quinn, Montreal Alouettes, 1954.

PASSES CAUGHT
- 13   Red O'Quinn, Montreal Alouettes, 1954.

YARDS GAINED PASS-CATCHING
316   Red O'Quinn, Montreal Alouettes

LONGEST TOUCHDOWN RUN ON PASS
93 Yards   Red O'Quinn, Montreal Alouettes ,1954.

YARDS GAINED PASSING
508   Sam Etcheverry, Montreal Alouettes, 1955.

INDIVIDUAL — ALL GAMES (1909-1970)

POINTS SCORED
  30 Joe Krol, Hamilton Flying Wildcats, Toronto Argonauts (7 games).

TOUCHDOWNS
   5 Hal Patterson, Montreal Alouettes, Hamilton Tiger-Cats (5 games).

POINTS KICKED
  23 Don Sutherin, Hamilton Tiger-Cats, Ottawa Rough Riders (8 games).
      Pep Leadlay, Queen's University, Hamilton Tigers (6 games).

FIELD GOALS
   3 George Fraser, Ottawa Rough Riders (4 games).
      Gerry James, Winnipeg Blue Bombers (6 games).
      Ches McCance, Winnipeg Blue Bombers, Montreal Alouettes (8 games).

CONVERTS
  17 Don Sutherin, Hamilton Tiger-Cats, Ottawa Rough Riders (8 games).

SINGLES
  12 Hughie Gall, University of Toronto, Toronto Parkdale (3 games).

TOUCHDOWN PASSES THROWN
   8 Russ Jackson, Ottawa Rough Riders (4 games).
      Bernie Faloney, Edmonton Eskimos, Hamilton Tiger-Cats (7 games).

TOUCHDOWN PASSES CAUGHT
   4 Hal Patterson, Montreal Alouettes, Hamilton Tiger-Cats (5 games).

CUP FINALS PLAYED

9	John Barrow, Hamilton Tiger-Cats:	1957-1958-1959-1961-1962-1963-1964-1965-1967.
	Tommy Grant, Hamilton Tiger-Cats:	1957-1958-1959-1961-1962-1963-1964-1965-1967.
8	Zeno Karcz, Hamilton Tiger-Cats:	1957-1958-1959-1961-1962-1963-1964-1965.
	Angelo Mosca, Hamilton Tiger-Cats:	1958-1959.
	Ottawa Rough Riders:	1960.
	Hamilton Tiger-Cats:	1962-1963-1964-1965-1967.
	Don Sutherin, Hamilton Tiger-Cats:	1958-1961-1962-1963-1964-1965.
	Ottawa Rough Riders:	1968-1969.
	Ches McCance, Winnipeg Blue Bombers:	1937-1938-1939-1941-1945.
	Winnipeg RCAF-Bombers:	1942-1943.
	Montreal Alouettes:	1949.
	Mel Wilson, Winnipeg Blue Bombers:	1938-1939-1941-1945-1946-1947.
	Winnipeg RCAF-Bombers:	1942.
	Calgary Stampeders:	1949.
	Bert Iannone, Winnipeg RCAF-Bombers:	1942-1943.
	Winnipeg Blue Bombers:	1945-1946-1947.
	Calgary Stampeders:	1948-1949.
	Saskatchewan Roughriders:	1951.
	Jack Wedley, Toronto Argonauts:	1937-1938-1945-1946-1947-1950.
	St. Hyacinthe-Donnacona:	1944.
	Saskatchewan Roughriders:	1951.

CUP CHAMPIONSHIP TEAMS

7   Jack Wedley, Toronto Argonauts:

1937 (Argos 4 Winnipeg Blue Bombers 3).

1938 (Argos 30 Winnipeg Blue Bombers 7).

1944 (St. Hyacinthe-Donnacona 7 Hamilton Flying Wildcats 6).

1945 (Argos 35 Winnipeg Blue Bombers 0).

1946 (Argos 28 Winnipeg Blue Bombers 6).

1947 (Argos 10 Winnipeg Blue Bombers 9).

1950 (Argos 13 Winnipeg Blue Bombers 0).

TEAM — PASSING (1931-1970)

TOUCHDOWN PASSES (1 TEAM)
4   Ottawa Rough Riders, 1969.
Toronto Argonauts, 1946.

TOUCHDOWN PASSES (BOTH TEAMS)
5   Ottawa Rough Riders (4) Saskatchewan Roughriders (1) 1969.
Saskatchewan Roughriders (3) Ottawa Rough Riders (2) 1966.

PASSES ATTEMPTED (1 TEAM)
46   Winnipeg Blue Bombers, 1953.

PASSES ATTEMPTED (BOTH TEAMS)
69   Winnipeg Blue Bombers (46) Hamilton Tiger-Cats (23) 1953.

PASSES COMPLETED (1 TEAM)
30   Montreal Alouettes, 1955.

PASSES COMPLETED (BOTH TEAMS)
39   Winnipeg Blue Bombers (28) Hamilton Tiger-Cats (11) 1953.

PASSES INCOMPLETE (1 TEAM)
23   Montreal Alouettes, 1956.
Winnipeg RCAF-Bombers, 1943.

PASSES INCOMPLETE (BOTH TEAMS)
32   Montreal Alouettes (23) Edmonton Eskimos (9) 1956.

FEWEST PASSES ATTEMPTED (1 TEAM)
3   Toronto Argonauts, 1950.

FEWEST PASSES ATTEMPTED (BOTH TEAMS)
8   Ottawa Rough Riders (4) Toronto Balmy Beach (4) 1940.

PASSES INTERCEPTED (1 TEAM)
4   By Edmonton Eskimos against Montreal Alouettes, 1956.

PASSES INTERCEPTED (BOTH TEAMS)
6   By Edmonton Eskimos (4) Montreal Alouettes (2) 1956.

YARDS GAINED PASSING (1 TEAM)
508   Montreal Alouettes, 1955.

YARDS GAINED PASSING (BOTH TEAMS)
580 Montreal Alouettes (508) Edmonton Eskimos (72) 1955.

TEAM — SINGLE GAME (1909-1970)—
POINTS SCORED (1 TEAM)
54 Queen's University, 1923.
50 Edmonton Eskimos, 1956.

POINTS SCORED (BOTH TEAMS)
77 Edmonton Eskimos (50) Montreal Alouettes (27) 1956.

FEWEST POINTS SCORED (BOTH TEAMS)
7 Toronto Argonauts (4) Winnipeg Blue Bombers (3) 1937.
  Toronto Argonauts (4) Sarnia Imperials (3) 1933.

TOUCHDOWNS (1 TEAM)
9 Queen's University, 1923.
7 Edmonton Eskimos, 1956.
  Hamilton Tigers, 1913.

TOUCHDOWNS (BOTH TEAMS)
11 Edmonton Eskimos (7) Montreal Alouettes (4) 1956.

POINTS KICKED (1 TEAM)
11 Winnipeg Blue Bombers, 1958.
   Ottawa Rough Riders, 1941.
   University of Toronto, 1909.

POINTS KICKED (BOTH TEAMS)
19 Ottawa Rough Riders (11) Winnipeg Blue Bombers (8) 1941.

FIELD GOALS (1 TEAM)
3 Ottawa Rough Riders, 1941.

FIELD GOALS (BOTH TEAMS)
5 Ottawa Rough Riders (3) Winnipeg Blue Bombers (2) 1941.

CONVERTS (1 TEAM)
7 Queen's University, 1923.
5 Edmonton Eskimos, 1955.

CONVERTS (BOTH TEAMS)
8 Winnipeg Blue Bombers (4) Hamilton Tiger-Cats (4) 1958.
  Edmonton Eskimos (5) Montreal Alouettes (3) 1955.

SINGLES (1 TEAM)
10 University of Toronto, 1909.

SINGLES (BOTH TEAMS)
12 University of Toronto (7) Ottawa Senators (5) 1926.
   Hamilton Tigers (9) Regina Roughriders (3) 1929.

YARDS GAINED RUSHING (1 TEAM)
448 Edmonton Eskimos, 1956.

YARDS GAINED RUSHING (BOTH TEAMS)
639 Edmonton Eskimos (448) Montreal Alouettes (191) 1956.

FUMBLES (1 TEAM)
9 Sarnia Imperials, 1933.

FUMBLES (BOTH TEAMS)
10 Winnipeg Blue Bombers (6) Hamilton Tiger-Cats (4) 1957.
   Sarnia Imperials (9) Toronto Argonauts (1) 1933.

FUMBLES LOST (1 TEAM)
  5 Winnipeg Blue Bombers, 1957.

FUMBLES LOST (BOTH TEAMS)
  7 Winnipeg Blue Bombers (5) Hamilton Tiger-Cats (2) 1957.

PENALTIES (BOTH TEAMS)
 16 Hamilton Tiger-Cats (10) Winnipeg Blue Bombers (6) 1958.

PENALTIES (1 TEAM)
 10 Hamilton Tiger-Cats, 1958.
YARDS PENALIZED (1 TEAM)
 97 Hamilton Tiger-Cats, 1958.

YARDS PENALIZED (BOTH TEAMS)
136 Hamilton Tiger-Cats (97) Winnipeg Blue Bombers (39) 1958.

PUNTS (1 TEAM)
 36 Hamilton Tigers, 1915.
     Toronto R&AA, 1915.

PUNTS (BOTH TEAMS)
 72 Hamilton Tigers (36) Toronto R&AA (36) 1915.

FEWEST PUNTS (1 TEAM)
  3 Montreal Alouettes, 1954.

FEWEST PUNTS (BOTH TEAMS)
 12 Edmonton Eskimos (6) Montreal Alouettes (6) 1955.

POINTS SCORED ONE QUARTER (1 TEAM)
 25 Toronto Argonauts, 1938 (4th).

POINTS SCORED ONE QUARTER (BOTH TEAMS)
 34 Winnipeg Blue Bombers (21) Hamilton Tiger-Cats (13) 1962 (2nd)

TOUCHDOWNS ONE QUARTER (1 TEAM)
  4 Toronto Argonauts, 1938 (4th)
     Queen's University, 1923 (3rd)
     Hamilton Tigers, 1913 (4th)

TOUCHDOWNS ONE QUARTER (BOTH TEAMS)
  5 Winnipeg Blue Bombers (3) Hamilton Tiger-Cats (2) 1962 (2nd)

GREY CUP TOUCHDOWN PASSES

The forward pass was legalized by the Canadian Rugby Union in 1931. Since that year, 66 touchdown passes have been thrown in Grey Cup finals.

Here is the year-by-year record:

1931 (1): Warren Stevens, Montreal Winged Wheelers, to Kennie Grant. Montreal defeated Regina Roughriders 22-0.

1934 (1): Oke Olson, Regina, to Steve Adkins. Sarnia Imperials defeated Regina Roughriders 20-12.

1935 (2): Russ Rebholz, Winnipegs, to Bud Marquardt and Greg Kabat. Winnipegs defeated Hamilton Tigers 18-12.

1938 (1): Bill Stukus, Toronto, to Bernie Thornton. Toronto Argonauts defeated Winnipeg Blue Bombers 30-7.

1939 (1): Orville Burke, Ottawa, to Tommy Daley who lateralled to Andy Tommy. Winnipeg Blue Bombers defeated Ottawa Rough Riders 8-7.

1941 (1): Wayne Sheley, Winnipeg, to Bud Marquardt who lateralled to Mel Wilson. Winnipeg Blue Bombers defeated Ottawa Rough Riders 18-16.

1942 (1): Wayne Sheley, Winnipeg, to Lloyd Boivin. Toronto RCAF-Hurricanes beat Winnipeg RCAF-Bombers 8-5.
1943 (2): Joe Krol, Hamilton, to Doug Smith. Brian Quinn, Winnipeg, to Dave Berry. Hamilton Flying Wildcats defeated Winnipeg RCAF-Bombers 23-14.
1944 (1): Dutch Davey, St. Hyacinthe-Donnacona, to Johnny Taylor. St. Hyacinthe defeated Hamilton Flying Wildcats 7-6.
1945 (2): Joe Krol, Toronto, to Doug Smylie and to Frank Hickey. Toronto Argonauts defeated Winnipeg Blue Bombers 35-0.
1946 (4): Joe Krol, Toronto, to Royal Copeland, Rod Smylie and Boris Tipoff. Royal Copeland to Joe Krol. Toronto Argonauts defeated Winnipeg Blue Bombers 28-6.
1947 (1): Joe Krol, Toronto, to Royal Copeland. Toronto Argonauts defeated Winnipeg Blue Bombers 10-9.
1948 (1): Keith Spaith, Calgary, to Normie Hill. Calgary Stampeders defeated Ottawa Rough Riders 12-7.
1949 (1): Frank Filchock, Montreal, to Bob Cunningham. Montreal Alouettes defeated Calgary Stampeders 28-15.
1951 (3): Tom O'Malley, Ottawa, to Alton Baldwin and Pete Karpuk. Glenn Dobbs, Saskatchewan, to Jack Nix. Ottawa Rough Riders defeated Saskatchewan Roughriders 21-14.
1952 (1): Nobby Wirkowski, Toronto, to Zeke O'Connor. Toronto Argonauts defeated Edmonton Eskimos 21-11.
1953 (1): Ed Songin, Hamilton, to Vito Ragazzo. Hamilton Tiger-Cats defeated Winnipeg Blue Bombers 12-6.
1954 (4): Sam Etcheverry, Montreal, two to Red O'Quinn, one to Joey Pal. Rollie Miles, Edmonton, to Earl Lindley. Edmonton Eskimos defeated Montreal Alouettes 26-25.
1955 (3): Jackie Parker, Edmonton, to Bob Haydenfeldt. Sam Etcheverry, Montreal, two to Hal Patterson. Edmonton Eskimos defeated Montreal Alouettes 34-19.
1956 (2): Sam Etcheverry, Montreal, to Hal Patterson. Don Getty, Edmonton, to Jackie Parker. Edmonton Eskimos defeated Montreal Alouettes 50-27.
1957 (1): Cliff Roseborough, Winnipeg, to Dennis Mendyk. Hamilton Tiger-Cats defeated Winnipeg Blue Bombers 32-7.
1958 (3): Leo Lewis, Winnipeg, to Jim Van Pelt. Bernie Faloney, Hamilton, two to Ron Howell. Winnipeg Blue Bombers defeated Hamilton Tiger-Cats 35-28.
1959 (1): Kenny Ploen, Winnipeg, to Ernie Pitts. Winnipeg Blue Bombers defeated Hamilton Tiger-Cats 21-7.
1960 (2): Russ Jackson, Ottawa, to Bill Sowalski. Jackie Parker, Edmonton, to Jim Letcavits. Ottawa Rough Riders defeated Edmonton Eskimos 16-6.
1961 (2): Bernie Faloney, Hamilton, to Paul Dekker and Ralph Goldston. Winnipeg Blue Bombers defeated Hamilton Tiger-Cats 21-14.
1962 (3): Leo Lewis, Winnipeg, to Charlie Shepard. Kenny Pleon, Winnipeg, to Farrell Funston who lateralled to Leo Lewis. Joe Zuger, Hamilton, to Dave Viti. Winnipeg Blue Bombers defeated Hamilton Tiger-Cats 28-27.
1963 (3): Bernie Faloney, Hamilton, to Willie Bethea and Hal Patterson. Joe Kapp, British Columbia Lions, to Mac Burton. Hamilton Tiger-Cats defeated British Columbia 21-10.
1964 (3): Bernie Faloney, Hamilton, to Tommy Grant and Stan Crisson. Pete Ohler, British Columbia Lions, to Jim Carphin. British Columbia defeated Hamilton 34-24.
1965 (1): Joe Zuger, Hamilton, to Willie Bethea. Hamilton Tiger-Cats defeated Winnipeg Blue Bombers 22-16.

196

1966 (5): Ron Lancaster, Saskatchewan, to Jim Worden, Alan Ford and Hugh Campbell. Russ Jackson, Ottawa, two to Whit Tucker. Saskatchewan Roughriders defeated Ottawa Rough Riders 29-14.
1967 (1): Joe Zuger, Hamilton, to Ted Watkins. Hamilton Tiger-Cats defeated Saskatchewan Roughriders 24-1.
1968 (3): Pete Liske, Calgary, two to Terry Evanshen. Russ Jackson, Ottawa, to Gene Adkins. Ottawa Rough Riders defeated Calgary Stampeders 24-21.
1969 (5): Russ Jackson, two to Ron Stewart, one each to Jay Roberts and Jim Mankins. Ron Lancaster, Saskatchewan, to Alan Ford. Ottawa Rough Riders defeated Saskatchewan Roughriders 29-11.

Touchdown passes have not been thrown in only six Grey Cup finals since the forward pass was legalized by the Canadian Rugby Union in 1931. They are:
1932: Hamilton Tigers 25 Regina Roughriders 6.
1933: Toronto Argonauts 4 Sarnia Imperials 3.
1936: Sarnia Imperials 26 Ottawa Rough Riders 20.
1937: Toronto Argonauts 4 Winnipeg Blue Bombers 3.
1940: Ottawa Rough Riders 20 Toronto Balmy Beach 7. (Two game total-point Cup final).
1950: Toronto Argonauts 13 Winnipeg Blue Bombers 0.

GREY CUP STANDINGS
(1909-1970)

	Played	Won	Lost	Points For	Points Against
Toronto	13	10	3	196	82
Hamilton	18	10	8	362	240
Ottawa	12	7	5	208	160
Winnipeg	19	7	12	223	352
Edmonton	7	3	4	128	144
Montreal	6	3	3	132	146
British Columbia	2	1	1	44	45
Calgary	3	1	2	48	59
Saskatchewan	11	1	10	82	264

Standings of Teams no longer in Cup Playoffs Ontario Rugby Football Union
(1909-1954)

	Played	Won	Lost	Points For	Points Against
Sarnia Imperials	3	2	1	48	36
Toronto Balmy Beach	4	2	2	30	43
Hamilton Alerts	1	1	0	11	4
Toronto RCAF-Hurricanes	1	1	0	8	5
Hamilton Wildcats	2	1	1	29	21
Toronto R&AA	1	0	1	7	13
Toronto Parkdale	2	0	2	8	70

Intercollegiate
(1909-1935)

	Played	Won	Lost	Points For	Points Against
Toronto	6	4	2	81	47
Queen's	3	3	0	78	4

197

The Grey Cup: A Statistical Summary

Year	Date	Place	Winner	Score	Loser	Score	Attendance	Receipts Gate	Winning Coach	Losing Coach	Field—Weather
1909	Dec. 4	Toronto	Tor U	26	Tor Parkdale	6	3,800	$ 2,616.40	Harry Griffith	Ed Livingstone	Good—Cloudy
1910	Nov. 26	Hamilton	Tor U	16	Ham Tigers	7	12,000	9,500.00	Harry Griffith	Sepi DuMoulin	Muddy—Overcast
1911	Nov. 25	Toronto	Tor U	14	Tor Argos	7	13,687	14,233.00	Dr. A. B. Wright	Billy Foulds	Frozen—Snow
1912	Nov. 30	Hamilton	Ham Alerts	11	Tor Argos	4	5,337	3,491.50	Liz Marriott	Jack Newton	Good—Clear
1913	Nov. 29	Hamilton	Ham Tigers	44	Tor Parkdale	2	2,100	1,993.75	Liz Marriott	Ed Livingstone	Slippery—Overcast
1914	Dec. 5	Toronto	Tor Argos	14	Tor U	2	10,500	8,150.00	Billy Foulds	Hugh Gall	Good—Cloudy
1915	Nov. 20	Toronto	Ham Tigers	13	Toronto R&AA	7	2,868	1,887.50	Liz Marriott	Ed Livingstone	Greasy—Rainy
1916-19	No Games, War										
1920	Dec. 4	Toronto	Tor U	16	Tor Argos	3	10,088	10,038.00	Mike Rodden	Laddie Cassels	Muddy—Rain
1921	Dec. 3	Toronto	Tor Argos	23	Edm Eskimos	0	9,558	9,991.30	Sinc McEvenue	Deacon White	Good—Snowflurries
1922	Dec. 2	Kingston	Queen's U	13	Edm Elks	1	4,700	4,839.00	Billy Hughes	Deacon White	Frozen—Clear
1923	Dec. 1	Toronto	Queen's U	54	Regina Roughriders	0	8,629	8,746.65	Billy Hughes	Jack Eddis	Good—Overcast
1924	Nov. 29	Toronto	Queen's U	11	Tor Balmy Beach	3	5,978	5,797.40	Billy Hughes	M. Rodden-A Buett	Muddy—Cloudy
1925	Dec. 5	Ottawa	Ott Senators	24	Wpg Tigers	1	6,900	6,000.00	Dave McCann	Harold Roth	Muddy—Rain
1926	Dec. 4	Toronto	Ott Senators	10	Tor U	7	8,276	9,063.15	Dave McCann	Ron McPherson	Frozen—Snowflurries
1927	Nov. 26	Toronto	Tor B. Beach	9	Ham Tigers	6	13,676	14,368.55	Dr. Harry Hobbs	Mike Rodden	Muddy—Rain
1928	Dec. 1	Hamilton	Ham Tigers	30	Regina Roughriders	0	4,767	5,738.71	Mike Rodden	Howie Milne	Muddy—Overcast
1929	Nov. 30	Hamilton	Ham Tigers	14	Regina Roughriders	3	1,906	2,537.42	Mike Rodden	Al Ritchie	Frozen—Snow
1930	Dec. 6	Toronto	Tor B. Beach	11	Regina Roughriders	6	3,914	4,066.50	Alex Ponton	Al Ritchie	Muddy—Rain
1931	Dec. 5	Montreal	Montreal AAA	22	Regina Roughriders	0	5,112	5,286.42	Clary Foran	Al Ritchie	Frozen—Snow
1932	Dec. 3	Hamilton	Ham Tigers	25	Regina Roughriders	6	4,806	3,873.65	Billy Hughes	Al Ritchie	Good—Cloudy
1933	Dec. 9	Sarnia	Tor Argos	4	Sarnia Imperials	3	2,751	3,187.48	Lew Hayman	Pat Oullette	Frozen—Snowflurries
1934	Nov. 24	Toronto	Sarnia Imps	20	Regina	12	8,900	6,396.11	Art Massucci	Greg Grassick	Good—Overcast
1935	Dec. 7	Hamilton	Winnipegs	18	Ham Tigers	12	6,405	5,583.92	Bob Fritz	Fred Veale	Muddy—Rainy
1936	Dec. 5	Toronto	Sarnia Imps	26	Ottawa	20	5,883	4,329.15	Art Massucci	Billy Hughes	Frozen—Cloudy
1937	Dec. 11	Toronto	Tor Argos	4	Wpg Bombers	3	11,522	11,585.25	Lew Hayman	Bob Fritz	Frozen—Snowflurries
1938	Dec. 10	Toronto	Tor Argos	30	Wpg Bombers	7	18,778	17,545.75	Lew Hayman	Reg Threlfall	Good—Cloudy
1939	Dec. 9	Ottawa	Wpg Bombers	8	Ottawa	7	11,738	11,468.95	Reg Threlfall	Ross Trimble	Frozen—Snowy
1940	Nov. 30	Toronto	Ottawa	8	Toronto B. Beach	2	4,993	3,925.50	Ross Trimble	Alex Ponton	Snowy—Clear
1940	Dec. 7	Ottawa	Ottawa	12	Toronto B. Beach	5	1,700	1,798.00	Ross Trimble	Alex Ponton	Muddy—Snow

(Ottawa won two-game total-point series 20-7)

Year	Date	City	Team 1	Score 1	Team 2	Score 2	Attendance	Receipts	Winning Coach	Losing Coach	Weather
1941	Nov. 29	Toronto	Wpg Bombers	18	Ottawa	16	19,065	17,592.75	Reg Threlfall	Ross Trimble	Good—Overcast
1942	Dec. 5	Toronto	Tor Hurricanes	8	Wpg RCAF-Bmers	5	12,455	9,257.00	Lew Hayman	Reg Threlfall	Slippery—Snow
1943	Nov. 27	Toronto	Ham Wildcats	23	Wpg RCAF-Bmers	14	16,423	14,695.25	Brian Timmis	Reg Threlfall	Good—Overcast
1944	Nov. 25	Hamilton	Mtl St. Hyacinthe	7	Ham Wildcats	6	3,871	3,425.00	Glen Brown	Eddie McLean	Good—Overcast
1945	Dec. 1	Toronto	Tor Argos	35	Wpg Bombers	0	18,660	17,492.25	Ted Morris	Bert Warwick	Snowy—Clear
1946	Nov. 30	Toronto	Tor Argos	28	Wpg Bombers	6	18,960	19,718.70	Ted Morris	Jack West	Good—Overcast
1947	Nov. 29	Toronto	Tor Argos	10	Wpg Bombers	9	18,885	25,459.50	Ted Morris	Jack West	Frozen—Clear
1948	Nov. 27	Toronto	Calgary	12	Ottawa	7	20,013	26,655.00	Les Lear	Wally Masters	Good—Overcast
1949	Nov. 26	Toronto	Montreal Als	28	Calgary	15	20,087	47,287.00	Lew Hayman	Les Lear	Muddy—Snow
1950	Nov. 25	Toronto	Tor Argos	13	Wpg Bombers	0	27,101	65,622.00	Frank Clair	Frank Larson	Mud—Slush—Cloudy
1951	Nov. 24	Toronto	Ottawa	21	Saskatchewan	14	27,341	115,184.56	Clem Crowe	Black Jack Smith	Good—Clear
1952	Nov. 29	Toronto	Tor Argos	21	Edm Eskimos	11	27,391	115,867.68	Frank Clair	Frank Filchock	Good—Clear
1953	Nov. 28	Toronto	Ham Tiger-Cats	12	Wpg Bombers	6	27,313	126,940.60	Carl Voyles	George Trafton	Good—Clear
1954	Nov. 27	Toronto	Edm Eskimos	26	Montreal Als	25	27,321	126,748.72	Frank Ivy	Doug Walker	Good—Clear
1955	Nov. 26	Vancouver	Edm Eskimos	34	Montreal Als	19	39,417	197,182.91	Frank Ivy	Doug Walker	Good—Overcast
1956	Nov. 24	Toronto	Edm Eskimos	50	Montreal Als	27	27,425	215,322.50	Frank Ivy	Doug Walker	Good—Clear
1957	Nov. 30	Toronto	Ham Tiger-Cats	32	Wpg Bombers	7	27,349	218,162.50	Jim Trimble	Bud Grant	Good—Clear
1958	Nov. 29	Vancouver	Wpg Bombers	35	Ham Tiger-Cats	28	36,567	293,062.50	Bud Grant	Jim Trimble	Good—Clear
1959	Nov. 28	Toronto	Wpg Bombers	21	Ham Tiger-Cats	7	33,133	302,628.50	Bud Grant	Jim Trimble	Slippery—Overcast
1960	Nov. 26	Vancouver	Ottawa	16	Edmonton	6	36,592	318,359.50	Frank Clair	Eagle Keys	Good—Clear
1961	Dec. 2	Toronto	Wpg Bombers	21	Ham Tiger-Cats	14	32,651	302,189.00	Bud Grant	Jim Trimble	Good—Cold
1962	Dec. 1-2	Toronto	Wpg Bombers	28	Ham Tiger-Cats	27	32,655	302,489.00	Bud Grant	Jim Trimble	Good—Fog
1963	Nov. 30	Vancouver	Ham Tiger-Cats	21	B.C. Lions	10	36,545	341,576.50	Ralph Sazio	Dave Skrien	Good—Cloudy
1964	Nov. 28	Toronto	B.C. Lions	34	Ham Tiger-Cats	24	32,655	305,443.00	Dave Skrien	Ralph Sazio	Slippery—Overcast
1965	Nov. 27	Toronto	Ham Tiger-Cats	22	Wpg Bombers	16	32,655	305,663.00	Ralph Sazio	Bud Grant	Good—Winds
1966	Nov. 26	Vancouver	Saskatchewan	29	Ottawa	14	36,553	341,975.50	Eagle Keys	Frank Clair	Slippery—Clear
1967	Dec. 2	Ottawa	Ham Tiger-Cats	24	Saskatchewan	1	31,358	332,960.00	Ralph Sazio	Eagle Keys	Hard—Cold
1968	Nov. 30	Toronto	Ottawa	24	Calgary	21	33,135	360,000.00	Frank Clair	Eagle Keys	Slippery—Cold
1969	Nov. 30	Montreal	Ottawa	29	Saskatchewan	11	33,172	405,000.00	Frank Clair	Eagle Keys	Hard—Cold